▼

RIGHT-
BRAIN
SEX

▲

RIGHT-BRAIN SEX

*Using Creative Visualization
to Enhance Sexual Pleasure*

CAROL G. WELLS

PRENTICE
HALL
PRESS

NEW YORK LONDON TORONTO SYDNEY TOKYO SINGAPORE

Prentice Hall Press
15 Columbus Circle
New York, New York 10023

Copyright © 1989 by Carol G. Wells

PRENTICE HALL PRESS and colophon are registered trademarks of Simon & Schuster, Inc.

Library of Congress Cataloging-in-Publication Data

Wells, Carol G.
Right-brain sex.

Includes bibliographical references.
1. Sex instruction. 2. Sex (Psychology). 3. Cerebral
dominance. I. Title.
HQ31.W472 1989   613.9′6   89-22811
ISBN 0-13-780818-6

Designed by Robert Bull Design

Manufactured in the United States of America

▼

Acknowledgments

▲

I wish to thank the following people:

Jon K. Meyer, M.D., my professor and mentor, who introduced me to the field of sexology and whose belief in me gave me the opportunity to explore this uncharted field.

My mother, Ida Rose Garonzik, from whom I learned discipline, determination, and perseverance.

My agent, Aaron Priest, who took a chance on an unknown writer and skillfully guided me through the uncertainties of being a rookie.

My editor, Marilyn Abraham, whose delicate balance of encouragement and criticism turned a usually painful process into a nurturing one.

My son, Greg, for always being himself in spite of having a sex therapist for a mom.

▼

Contents

▲

Contents

Are you having trouble concentrating during sex? Techniques that help

Contents

▼

Preface

▲

Of all the many things I like about being a sex therapist, the one that gives me most satisfaction is providing an environment in which people feel comfortable talking about their sexual concerns. I know when people walk through my door they are both scared and relieved. It's scary to tell someone your deepest secrets, especially the sexual ones. But it's also very healing to unburden—to share what you alone have been harboring.

The people who come through my doors are from all walks of life: realtors, bank presidents, longshoremen, homemakers, secretaries, teachers, and computer geniuses. They range in age from sixteen through eighty. They've been married, single, and divorced—sometimes divorced many times. They've all been different, but they all share something in common: a desire to have sexual happiness.

The reasons for being unhappy are many. Some have problems with their bodies not cooperating with their minds. They feel very aroused but find they can't orgasm, or orgasm too quickly, or they can't get an erection. Some have problems with their minds not cooperating with their bodies. They can get aroused, but they don't seem interested. To them, sex seems like a lot of work.

Some of the patients I see have experienced a great

deal of pain and trauma in their lives whereas others have had normal, happy lives. Yet, no matter what their biographies, the one common denominator is that sex somehow does not feel like "second nature" to them. They're just not totally comfortable with the thoughts, sensations, bodily feelings, or emotions surrounding sexuality. Of course, the truth is that very few of us are totally comfortable with our sexuality; most have a vulnerability or two . . . or three.

I applaud my patients for their courage to seek greater happiness. No matter how "modern" we think we are, sex is still a source of much embarrassment and shame. So I appreciate the strength it takes to admit to oneself that it "ain't going so well" and then to take the extra step of fortitude to seek outside help.

But most of all, I appreciate the lessons my patients have taught me: That it's worth the effort to try to make it better. That revealing is truly healing. That men and women struggle equally with sexual discomfort. That everyone makes mistakes. That change is never easy. That there are rarely simple answers to complex problems. That some problems don't have answers. And last, but certainly not least, that it's never too late to find happiness.

▼

Introduction

▲

As a marriage counselor and sex therapist, the question I am asked most often is: What is the most frequent sexual complaint of couples? Almost without exception, the answer produces a familiar sigh from the inquirer. The answer, as true a hundred years ago as it is today, is boredom.

Most of us think of boredom as coming from outside ourselves: too much exposure to the same thing over and over. It could be a job, a daily routine, or a person. Given that most of us think of it in this way, it's only natural that we look outside ourselves for change. With sexual boredom, we often think about new partners as a solution. Many of us have even tried this solution.

Today the option of dealing with boredom by changing partners has been drastically reduced. The deadly malady called AIDS (acquired immunodeficiency syndrome) has caused us to reexamine more closely how to make long-term sexual relationships satisfying. This book is for the single, the married, the men, and the women who wish to find that satisfaction. Following the advice in this book will assist you in relieving sexual boredom, establishing a new sexual closeness and warmth, and also in overcoming specific sexual dysfunctions.

What follows may surprise you. As you look at the titles of the chapters, you'll notice their basic simplicity:

touch, pleasure, lust, play, and feeling loved. Could the answers to long-term sexual happiness really be contained in such "old-fashioned" concepts? And if it's so simple and basic, why do so few of us have it?

The answer is that too often we look outside ourselves for happiness. This book is about going inside ourselves to find the answers. By using our own creativity, located in our right brain, we can enhance our sexual joy. The key to sexual satisfaction has always been in "our own backyard," we've just never known it was so close and so easy to access.

In recent years, there has been much written about the possibilities of two distinct hemispheres of our brain. The left brain, which is responsible for the more practical, analytical part of us, and the right brain, which is responsible for the more ethereal, imaginative part. Because our right brain is proposed to be the center of imagery, it contains all the sexual images we've collected over a lifetime. Without knowing it, these images guide our sexual behavior and determine our sexual happiness. Be prepared in the pages that follow to unearth some buried notions about your sexuality. The discovery of hidden images frees us to explore new options for greater sexual happiness.

The path to discovery will be paved by a simple process called visualization. Visualization is goal-directed imagery. We direct our minds toward a certain purpose. In the past, visualization has mainly been used to improve performance in business or sports. A public speaker or a skier visualizes a perfect performance before attempting the real thing. They're using imagery to accomplish a goal. *Right-Brain Sex* shows you how to use visualization to achieve the goal of enhancing your sexual satisfaction.

Visualization allows us to go on unchartered journeys through the Amazon of our minds where we will find quixotic adventures never before experienced. On this journey we will learn to use visualization to expand our sexual choices. *Our mind is the most powerful of all our sex organs.* By learning to use its full erotic potential, our sex lives can be dramatically changed.

The use of visualization in my practice as a sex therapist came to me (as many things do in life) out of a need to solve a problem. My single and divorced patients felt they would never be able to solve their problems if they didn't have a partner. How could they get better if they couldn't "practice" with another person? Surrogate partners, in my opinion, present as many problems as solutions.

The answer came in the form of imaginary partners. Because visualization allows mental rehearsal in anticipation of the real-life experience, it allowed my patients to practice before they had to participate. As you will learn by reading this book, visualization has proven effective in doing just that.

My use of visualization started out as a way to help with a specific situation and ended up changing my whole way of thinking. As I increasingly used visualization with individuals and couples, I increasingly realized its potential. I moved from the specific to the general and came to understand that visualization has the power to move us past our own internal blocks into limitless boundaries. The importance of this notion in dealing with sexuality had a powerful impact on me.

Visualization allows us to get in touch with our unconscious. Once beyond our fixed boundaries, we have the opportunity to explore our full potential. With visualization we can produce, direct, and act out our own sexual scripts, changing them whenever we need to.

The big advantage of being able to change our sexual

scenarios is that we don't get bored. We introduce novelty by using our imagination. Equally important is that visualization also allows us to rid ourselves of sexual inhibitions as well as sexual failures.

Because each of us have a unique history, we have our own personal sexual imagery that has been implanted, nurtured, and developed from early infancy to young adulthood. Our sexual images run deep and for the most part are out of our awareness and yet have a powerful influence on our behavior. The unconscious exerts so much control over us because we are not aware of making choices when we operate on an unconscious level—our actions seem to be occurring automatically.

The individuals and couples I work with in therapy are universally surprised at the power of their unconscious images, especially the sexual ones. In most cases, they feel helpless to change the images that are causing problems. The helplessness remains until they become consciously aware of how they are being influenced by their images.

For example, I remember a couple who were making remarkable progress in therapy. They decided to go on a romantic vacation to celebrate their reunion with great sex. They chose a remote island with an option of hideaway cottages. Perfect—they thought. There was a hitch, however. Outside the cottage, they felt very sexy, whispering erotic suggestions to each other. Once inside the cottage, they both lost all sexual desire and even found themselves irritable. Their frustration mounted and I received a frantic call.

I asked them both to do a visualization exercise. They were to close their eyes, really concentrate on the inside of the cottage and then let their minds freely associate to another room in their past. What they both discovered was that the cottage room reminded them of her parents' guest house where they first had sex. Her father had walked in on them, causing great embarrassment, guilt, and, of course, sexual failure. Until that day, they thought that incident was well behind them. Once they moved from their rented cottage to the main hotel, they were able to begin their celebration.

This book will help you to discover your current sexual images and to change or expand these images in whatever direction you want. When you do so, you will find your behavior changing. It may be either a dramatic change or a slower, less obvious but equally important change. In spite of the power of visualization, it is not magic. You arrived at your current images from years and years of repeated input. The concepts and exercises presented in this book must be regularly practiced in order for you to benefit from them.

What's really exciting about visualization is that you can travel to adventurous and new places. If you allow yourself the freedom to do so, visualization can make your sex life come alive and stay alive—for as long as you're willing to explore the various creative images of your mind. It will be a trip well worth your efforts.

In my home I have a sun room with a skylight. I have filled the room with plants and a garden fountain. This is where I take my trips. I close my eyes, let the image of a forest and a stream come to mind, focus on my breathing, and let my mind go on whatever trip I have designed for myself. The possibilities never end.

► CHAPTER 1

Visualization— What It Is and What It Can Do for Your Sex Life

▼

Visualization is part imagination, part meditation, and part analogy. The purpose of visualization is to facilitate change. It is a remarkably simple process that anybody can do. Prove it to yourself right now. After reading the following instructions, give it a try.

1. Say the following three words to yourself until you have them memorized: *imagination, meditation, analogy.*
2. Close your eyes.
3. Take five very deep, slow breaths, letting your body relax more and more with each breath.
4. Now, in your mind's eye, visualize a blackboard with a large circle on it. Divide that circle into three equal parts so that it becomes a pie—as you did when you were first learning fractions in math.
5. Go around the pie and in each part put one of the three words: *imagination, meditation, analogy.*
6. Keep that image in your mind by going around the circle three times, each time visualizing and saying the words to yourself.
7. Erase the circle from the blackboard and open your eyes.

Congratulations! You have successfully done visualization. You have also committed to your mind, exactly what visualization is: imagination, meditation, and analogy. Now combine it with relaxation (which you did by breathing deeply) and direct it toward a specific goal (committing to memory the three words), and you have all the elements of visualization. Remember, it's very simple and you've changed because you've learned something new.

Imagination is the key element in visualization. The reason it is so important is because it acts as a shortcut—a picture is worth a thousand words. By experimenting with the directed images in this book, your unconscious will "get the message" much faster than if you tried to "talk" to it through words. For example, if you are upset, the common solution is to tell yourself to relax. You give yourself a command, "relax!" It usually doesn't work. Instead, if you imagine yourself alone, luxuriating in the warm afternoon sun on the beach with the sounds of the sea all around you, you will automatically relax. This is how you use visualization to create change.

The meditation part implies that visualization has a trancelike, contemplative quality. It is a state of intense concentration. During visualization you will be blocking out all distractions. You will go into yourself and concentrate on only the immediate task—using your imagination. Anybody can meditate. It's something we do all the time. Think about how often you've been driving in your car and find you've been so concentrated you forgot to make a turn or take your exit.

The last part of visualization involves analogies or comparisons of similarities. Because they involve images, analogies help us more quickly understand certain thoughts and feelings that don't lend themselves to easy expression. You might be familiar with the analogy that the personality is like an onion. It has a multitude of layers that can be peeled away to reveal the core. The imagery gives us a familiar picture that facilitates our understanding.

The act of sex (intercourse) is something we are able to picture. Now try to get a picture of your sexuality. Sexuality is abstract and vague and much more difficult to understand. Yet, sexual happiness consists of much more than the act of sex. To have long-lasting sexual happiness, you need to understand and be comfortable with your sexuality. Through the use of imagery, meditation, and analogy, this book will help you to get a comfortable picture of your sexuality.

Visualization and Your Right Brain

The right side of the brain is considered to be the seat of passion, dreams, intuition, and images. Because it is holistic, it sees things all at once. The left side of our brain is thought to be more logical, rational, mathematical, and is the seat of reason. It sees things one at a time. Visualization and its relatives dreams, fantasies, hypnosis, and flow states are all right-brain activities.

Dreaming is visualization in the unconscious state. Current dream research tells us much about the value of visualization. Our dreams are purposefully directed, and during times of stress they help us find solutions. Ongoing research is even looking at the possibility that individuals can manipulate their dreams toward a certain goal.

One research project asks the person to design a more successful outcome for troublesome dreams, it is hoped that some of the new solutions will actually impact waking behavior. Early results with this research have shown that people can wake up during a frustrating dream, decide to change the ending, and then reenter the same dream adding the new ending. Although all of this is still very much in the research phase, there is no doubt that dreams help to alleviate stress.

The difference between fantasy and visualization is that fantasy is not directed toward a specific purpose. It's more free floating and doesn't involve analogies. Sexual fantasies contain erotic images; visualizations can be non-erotic even though designed to achieve a specific sexual goal. While sexual fantasy is very important to sexuality, you will notice immediately that the visualizations in this book do not in any way resemble sexual fantasies. In fact, very few of them contain any sexual or erotic images.

Hypnosis also has much in common with visualization. Hypnosis is an altered state of consciousness in which the brain waves are slowed down. During sleep we are unconscious and our brain waves are at their minimum, during consciousness they are at their maximum. In the hypnotic state, the brain waves are halfway in between. In this state we have access to both the conscious and unconscious mind.

Visualization is done during a relaxed state similar to hypnosis, but not as deep. In this relaxed place the mind has an opportunity to wander in a less-inhibited manner. A relaxed state filters out the overly stringent censor that exists in most of us. Without this censor, our mind can explore places we've never dared to adventure.

Research in something called "flow states" is also ongoing. Flow states exist when the mind is intensely concentrated and blocks out all distractions. Any irrelevant stimuli are ignored, such as the phone ringing or someone talking. Time is distorted—either stretched or more likely compressed. The most significant part of flow states is the feeling of absolute mastery—one actually expands the apparent limitations of the self. Athletes, artists, surgeons, and others whose work requires extreme concentration describe episodes of flow states.

Unfortunately, one cannot simply will oneself into a flow state. Learning to screen out distractions, however, allows one to move into a flow state. Orgasm occurs during a flow state. With practice, visualization can help a person tune out distractions and actually cultivate the ability to achieve the flow state necessary for orgasm.

Because intense concentration is so essential to athletic mastery, sports psychology has been looking into such concepts as flow states, inner calm, relaxation, and guided imagery—the components of visualization. Consequently, sports psychology has taught us the most about visualization. Recent evidence indicates that visualization is the core performance-enhancing strategy used in sports. Some sports psychologists believe that controlled visualization can induce the same brain waves one will use during the chosen activity, whether it's competitive skiing or public speaking. It's possible that visualization might even create a template or "road map" for performance that guides the physical and mental processes that occur during the actual event.

In this book you will read much about the importance of intense concentration needed during enjoyable sex. States of concentration that exist in dreams, hypnosis, flow states, and even athletic performance tell us much about how to achieve this concentration during sex.

Two Brains?

Research into the area of brain asymmetry is still very new. Consequently, the idea of two separate brains, each functioning independently of the other, has not been definitively proven. What does seem certain, however, is evidence supporting the existence of hemispheric differences. Although the exact nature of these differences is still being determined, early evidence has attributed the different mental processes as follows*:

LEFT HEMISPHERE	RIGHT HEMISPHERE
Intellect	Intuition
Convergent	Divergent
Deductive	Imaginative
Rational	Metaphoric
Vertical	Horizontal
Discrete	Continuous
Abstract	Concrete
Realistic	Impulsive
Directed	Free
Differential	Existential
Sequential	Multiple
Historical	Timeless
Analytic	Holistic
Explicit	Tacit
Objective	Subjective
Successive	Simultaneous

It's not likely that the brain operates in such a simplistic, divided way. What's more probable is a collaborative effort. However, for purposes of understanding the concepts described in this book, it is useful to think in terms of a division between the two sides of the brain. By using the analogy of two distinct brains, we can better understand the importance of needing to make a transition from our more

*Springer, Sally, and Deutsch, Georg. *Left Brain, Right Brain*. San Francisco, Calif.: W. H. Freeman and Co., 1981.

analytical, realistic, and objective parts of ourselves to our freer, timeless, and more imaginative parts. Great sex happens *only* when we're in touch with the latter.

How Visualization Bypasses Your Sexual Roadblocks

If you think about it, visualization is actually one of our earliest learning methods. As a newborn infant we learn a lot about the world through what we see. We don't learn words until many months later and it is years before we learn to read the written word. Unfortunately, once we have mastered the written and verbal word, we too often abandon the actual visual experience for the thinking about or analyzing of the experience.

Earlier I said our unconscious gets an image faster than it does words. That's because our foundation for understanding the world is visual. As an adult, returning to visualization to learn is both regressive and primitive. This actually helps us to learn because the ways and things we learn the earliest are deeply ingrained. They may get filed away but they never get completely forgotten.

The imagery in visualization reaches deep down into our earliest learning strategy and helps us to learn new thoughts and ideas about our sexuality. Rather than trying to unlearn problematic ideas, it's more like learning them for the first time. Using visualizations helps us ignore previous learning that may be causing current sexual problems.

The analogy in visualization helps to bypass roadblocks that keep us from changing. Analogies are a way for us to "see" things differently. For example, there is a book for women that contains many drawings that visually equate the female genitals with flowers. The imagery and analogy help women to think of their genitals as beautiful, delicate, and sweet-smelling.

Visualization not only taps into our earliest learning but it also taps into our creativity. In a world that demands many tedious, uncreative, and repetitious tasks, visualization is a refreshing change. Practicing visualization "exercises" our right brain, which is often overlooked in favor of reason, logic, and task accomplishment—all parts of our left brain. When we remain too long in our left brain, we eventually get bored.

How Using Your Right Brain Makes You Passionate and Overcomes Boredom

Boredom is the result of spending too much time in left-brain activity. Without the passion that comes from our intuitive, explorative self, boredom is inevitable. Few of us have escaped experiencing it at one time or another. Some of us live with chronic boredom.

Boredom is a feeling of uninvolvement, lack of contentment, loss of enthusiasm, absence of motivation, and feelings of emptiness. In short, a very distasteful bedfellow. When one is bored, there always seems to be a lack of goal direction. Nothing appeals to us and there is no excitement for what is happening. This lack of involvement is central to boredom because when one is operating in the right brain, involvement is so intense that it is impossible to be bored. Remember the flow state described above? Being in a flow state is the exact opposite of being bored.

Shamans and Science

Visualization is not a new concept. It has been traced back as far as ancient Egypt where the summoning and holding of certain images were used by shamans in many cultural rituals. In the last few decades, visualization has been approached more scientifically. Systematic visualization is increasingly being used to improve skills, especially in tasks requiring performance such as athletics, public speaking, and even productivity in business.

In fact, a study done by the National Research Council (NRC) concluded that mental imagery improves a variety of skills. The NRC conclusion was based on a review of hundreds of studies and two years of experience with workshops, laboratory visits, and commercially available self-improvement programs. The study found that practice is more likely to make perfect if combined with the imaging of the new tasks to be performed. Mental imaging was especially beneficial if the tasks to be done required a thoughtful, systematic approach.

It's important to distinguish boredom from its look-alike, depression. A person who is depressed also exhibits many of the same feelings listed above. The essential difference is that with depression, feelings of guilt, unworthiness, sinfulness, hopelessness, failure, and self-blame are also present.

Boredom exists in degrees and even a mild case is unpleasant. Unfortunately, boredom can also be difficult to recognize. That's because we live with so much of it all the time. Our world demands that we operate in our left brains far too much. It takes a great deal of energy and effort to counteract this.

Because we don't easily recognize boredom, we search for other alternatives for the unpleasant feelings. We feel angry and irritable. Not realizing that boredom may be causing our emotions, we look around for convenient scapegoats. Relationships are our most convenient target. We get angry with the people we love, the people we work with, our friends, and our neighbors. When we're bored at work, we may come home in a foul mood and get angry at the kids. When we're bored in a relationship, we pick fights or focus on small imperfections in our mate.

It's also true that people who are easily bored are afraid to take chances. They tend to lead a highly routinized daily life. They think routine provides security, but they are often unaware of the price they pay: boredom and its appendage, anger.

Psychological profiles of people who experience frequent boredom have shown that in addition to having a lot of routine in their life, consistently bored people are also overly concerned with pleasing others, prone to worry, lack confidence, depend too much on others, focus on material things, are overly conforming, and overly sensitive to criticism from self and others.

They tend to look outward for blame and engage in fantasies that consist of ''if only'': If only I were rich. If only I were famous. If only I had married Sue instead of Jane. If only I had stopped at two children instead of three. In searching outside themselves for solutions, they remain stuck in their own inability to take risks and their own fears of what uncertainty brings.

Visualization can help because it looks within yourself for help. You're using your own creativity to find a solution rather than blaming the outside world. Even though this book is about using visualization to overcome sexual hazards, visualization as a solution is certainly not limited to sex. Once you master the technique, you can use it in other areas of your life—to find a new hobby, a new direction to your career, or a new approach to your children.

How Bored Are You with Your Sex Life?

Boredom in relationships is probably the most extensive and serious challenge facing us. Our culture and family life is structured around monogamy. Monogamy, all too often, gets turned into monotony. The novelty factor in any relationship tends toward a decline the longer the relationship continues.

In new relationships we function mostly with our right brain. We feel challenged and the challenge leads to a lot of right-brain activity such as overwhelming passion and excitement. We go out a lot, stay up late, and still have lots of energy. At the peak of the romance curve, our sexual desire is hardly containable. We seem preoccupied by the other person and can't wait to see them again, even if we were just with them. As the challenge wanes, and the predictability rises, we tend toward operating in our left brain. Boredom starts to set in. We start analyzing the relationship, worrying about financial security, and finding fault. The passion dies. Sex diminishes or disappears.

At a level too dangerous for most of us to identify, we feel trapped. The trapped feeling comes from the belief that we don't have choices within the framework of the relationship. Our inability to take risks and our habituation toward routine deadens our creativity. We don't want to acknowledge our own responsibility for our behavior so we blame the people we depend on. Anger follows. Issues of right or wrong take over and differences become highlighted. The differences give credence to our anger and we feel justified. All of this serves to mask taking responsibility for our boredom.

As a therapist who deals with couples in the throes of bad times, I am continually confronted with resistance to innovation and change. A couple will complain about their lack of sexual contact and will explain in great detail the daily grind that keeps them from getting together. Often the creative, romantic suggestions I make are counteracted by a long list of "priority" tasks that need to be done. Doing the laundry on Saturday morning becomes more important than having breakfast in bed together. Watching television takes on greater importance than a moonlit walk. It's as if routine descends on us, takes hold, and just refuses to let go.

In fact, the "need" for routine is a cover-up, usually for the anger people feel toward the other person. Watching television or doing the laundry is a way to avoid contact. Avoidance is a natural human behavior toward people who are the object of our anger.

Remember, the whole process goes like this: boredom, then feeling trapped, then blame, then anger, then avoidance.

Because passionate sex is a right-brain activity and because most of us tend to operate much too often in the left brain, we easily get into trouble with our sexuality. When we allow our sexual activity to become too routine, we switch to our left brain. Eventually we will become bored. At this point we will find ourselves either losing interest in our partner or in sex. We may even find ourselves starting to have sexual problems such as impotency, early ejaculation, orgasm difficulty, or feelings of sexual aversion.

Solutions people use to counteract sexual boredom are often extreme. We lose interest in our partner, we get angry at them, we "put up" with an unexciting sexual life at home and seek "thrills" elsewhere. Because new relationships automatically bring our right brain into action, they seem easier than finding ways to stimulate right-brain activity with our current lovers.

Visualization provides a less drastic and more creative alternative. It allows us to "get in touch" with our right brain, ourselves, and our partners. The more we do this, the more passion we will put back into our lives. Instead of letting the passion dwindle, visualization can keep it alive.

Consider the following situation and rate yourself according to predictability. Give yourself a 5 if very predictable and a 1 if never predictable or rate yourself somewhere in between if appropriate. When you're finished, add up the score to determine your "Boredom Quotient."

1. The time of day we have sex   1 2 3 4 5
2. The day of the week we have sex   1 2 3 4 5
3. The place we have sex   1 2 3 4 5
4. Who initiates   1 2 3 4 5
5. How we get started   1 2 3 4 5
6. What we are wearing   1 2 3 4 5
7. What we do to arouse each other   1 2 3 4 5
8. The order of events   1 2 3 4 5
9. What we say or don't say during sex   1 2 3 4 5
10. What we do after we finish sex   1 2 3 4 5

This survey should give you some idea about how routine and predictable you've allowed your sex life to become. If your score is 30 or above, you're probably bored most of the time. You may not have needed a test to tell you this. The question is, are you willing to do something about it?

Are You Ready to Make a Change?

Dealing with boredom in relationships is not simple. That's because human beings are *never* simple. We have different parts of ourselves and each part can want something different. For example, we all have dependency needs to varying degrees. We also have a need to be autonomous and self-sufficient. This makes change a very complex process. The part of us that wants to be independent may want to do something about being bored, but the dependent part of us wants somebody else to take care of it. With this tug-of-war, it's easy to go nowhere.

Before anything will change, we have to acknowledge that our dependent child will naturally resist taking this kind of responsibility. Then, we have to give more strength to the side that wants change—the adult, autonomous part. It's not always easy to grow up and take that kind of responsibility. Remember when you were a small child playing with friends and something was broken? Instinctively and immediately you disclaimed any responsibility. The instinct seems to stay with us as we mature.

If you find yourself feeling very skeptical about the suggestions in this book, take a deep look inside yourself. Ask yourself: What could be the possible benefits of staying bored? Having someone else to blame? Not risking uncertainty by changing? It could be fear.

For example, a patient of mine who had been to several different sex therapists for his problem with early ejaculation found out his resistance to change through visualization. This is how it happened: I asked him to visualize a path. In this path was a huge boulder that was blocking his way to the other side where there were many riches to be had.

Then I asked him what he saw. He said he saw himself climbing up a mountain that was on one side of the path. On the mountain were lots of trees and he was using the trees to help pull himself up. He said the trees seemed to represent good memories. Then he said he felt himself being pulled back. When asked what was pulling him back, he said he was holding onto a woman. He was trying to pull her up the mountain but she kept holding him back. I asked him to let go of the woman, but he said he couldn't because she couldn't take care of herself—she would fall down.

We talked about the visualization experience afterward. Did he feel the need to take care of women? Yes, his mother was a very dependent woman. She divorced when he was nine and she seemed to fall apart and stayed that way until the present—always needing him in order to get along. His image of women is that they are all dependent. The fear that he would be engulfed by a dependent woman keeps him sexually dysfunctional. In spite of what appears to be an apparent paradox, my patient actually felt more secure being a sexual cripple. That way he had a "legitimate" excuse for not making a commitment to a woman.

The trees provided my patient with the answer to his dilemma. He needed to use the good memories in his life to help move him forward rather than focusing on the negative—his dependent mother. His future visualization exercises were centered around positive events with women who were not dependent, so he learned to see women as more multidimensional. As his images of women became more positive, he began making progress with his sexual problem.

That's how easily visualization can help you unlock your mind and open up a happier, healthier sex life. Are you ready for the adventure?

Guidelines for Doing Visualization

The visualizations in this book are designed for a specific reason. Each visualization is preceded by a statement of purpose. There is also an appendix that gives you a cross-reference to which visualizations are appropriate for which situations. If you find your particular situation is not mentioned, don't be discouraged. Once you've read this book, you'll be very familiar with how visualizations work and you can "customize" your own. Trust your own imagination and let your mind take you where your unconscious wants to go.

Here are some general guidelines to use when doing a visualization:

Set the mood. Mood is important. Special training, skill, personality, equipment, or time of day is not. You do need a quiet environment and five or ten minutes of unpressured, uninterrupted time. You will also need an open, experimental mind. And you will need to be *relaxed*.

Relaxation allows the brain waves to slow down so that you are more easily in touch with the unconscious. In this place, images will flow uncensored by the highly analytic conscious left-brain processes.

Concentrate. Concentration is also important. Concentration means staying focused on the task at hand and ignoring any distractions. If you know you have trouble concentrating, be sure you've read chapter 2. This chapter will help you learn to concentrate. Most people who haven't practiced visualization will find that, in the beginning, their mind will tend to wander. If it does, you can learn to bring it back into focus. If you find yourself getting frustrated by not being able to concentrate, please refresh your memory by reading chapter 2 again and practicing the concentration exercises.

Relax. Be sure you are in a comfortable chair, couch, or bed where your body is well supported. If you are especially tired, don't try visualization. You will probably just fall asleep. And although dreams are important to your psyche, they won't accomplish the same thing. Here's how to relax:

- Close your eyes and begin relaxing by focusing on your breathing; take ten very slow, deep breaths; breathe in through your nose, out through your mouth
- Count your breaths; if your mind wanders, just bring it back into focus; resume counting or start again; it doesn't matter
- When you have reached ten deep breaths, begin focusing on your body; visualize any tension in your body as a color; now visualize the tension vaporizing away from your body into the air around you; you will ''see'' the tension vaporize and your entire body will become limp and relaxed
- When you are relaxed, you can begin your visualization; if you're using one from the book, simply let it come to your mind; if you're creating your own, let your mind wander; it will settle on whatever is important

Practice. There is no substitute for it. Practice really does make perfect. Intermittent visualization is subject to the pitfalls of all intermittent learning: Nothing seems to change. On the other hand, the more you do visualization, the easier it will become. The changes you desire will occur more rapidly.

CHAPTER 2

Mastering Your Most Powerful Sexual Organ: Your Mind

▼

Three Right-Brain Processes Necessary for Really Great Sex

You've already learned that your sexual images have a great deal to do with sexual happiness. And you've learned that visualization is an effective way to change images. In this chapter you will learn how to master three right-brain processes necessary for really great sex: (1) change, (2) transitions, and (3) concentration.

Even though these don't sound very sexy, it's impossible to enhance your sexuality without having mastered all three. This is a how-to book and I'd be selling you short if I didn't tell you that to get what you want sexually, you have to do some mental rearranging. So if you're tempted to skip ahead—be warned! You won't make a difference in your life without having conquered the techniques in this chapter. Without mastering these, the visualizations won't be effective.

Strategies for Changing Your Sex Life

Why am I taking time to write about change in a book on sex? Because I don't want you to be frustrated. I want this book to make a difference in your life. It won't if you don't understand how change works. You'll read it, try a few visualizations, and if nothing dramatic happens, you'll put it aside, go on living with whatever you wanted to change, and eventually look for another how-to book. I know, because I used to do this with self-help books myself.

We all have many things in our lives we want to change. We want to be more patient parents, less obsessive about work, and more loving with our mates. In spite of our good intentions, we find change difficult to bring about. What makes it so difficult is that learning is easier than unlearning. In order to change, we have to dump, so to speak, the initial "wrong" learning before we can bring in new material. If we could just get it right the first time, life would be so much simpler.

An example is the three year old that went flying by me on the ski slopes while I was struggling to stay upright. She won't have to unlearn all the bad habits I battle with now. Incidentally, my ski instructor told me it takes twenty-one days of straight skiing to knock out one bad habit. I don't know how scientific her information is, but given I'm still doing all the wrong things, I'm inclined to believe her.

When it comes to sex, we learn a lot of "wrong" things. We're still pretty uptight when it comes to talking openly and honestly with our children about sexual pleasure. Because we say very little, sex remains secretive, setting the stage for negative emotions and images. After all, in a child's mind, you only keep a secret if you've done something wrong. As adults the "wrong" learning has to be "righted" if we're to find sexual happiness.

Visualization greatly facilitates this relearning process. Still, it takes time, energy, and lots of practice to make long-lasting changes. Here are some important strategies to keep in mind while you're working with the visualizations in this book.

Strategies to Change By

Change requires making trade-offs with your time. As simple as it sounds, you have to give up some of your time to learn something new. If it takes five minutes to do a visualization, that's five minutes you can't do something else. Most of us are pressed for time anyway, so finding another five minutes is not as easy as it sounds. Decide what you're willing to give up, five minutes of television or sleep, for example. Then make a commitment to yourself to make the sacrifice.

Break down desired change into small behaviors. Most people overwhelm themselves with vague goals. For example, ''I want to have better sex.'' This doesn't give you enough direction. What exactly do you want to be better? Do you want more touching? A different approach from your partner? More variety? Maybe you want them all. That's fine as long as you've identified specific *behaviors* that can be accomplished.

Work on each behavior one at a time. After you've listed your specific goals, prioritize them so you know where to start. If you don't, you'll end up overwhelmed and frustrated and unable to monitor your progress.

Be prepared to practice. This is where most people fall short. It's natural for motivation to wane when you don't experience immediate success. We're used to immediate rewards. It's tough to hang in there when we don't get quick results. However, change simply doesn't occur on the first attempt so be prepared to stay with it by practicing.

Use positive messages to motivate yourself. Never put yourself down for not making the desired change. Calling yourself lazy, stupid, foolish, or worse will feed the failure ''undertow.'' You'll be dragged down by your own negative energy. Use positive affirmations instead.

''I know I can do it'' and ''I deserve to have this in my life'' are examples of positive motivating statements.

Never underestimate the complexity of change. It's important to have a positive attitude about change while at the same time being realistic and patient about your expectations. This combination will get you the best results.

How Practice Helps Us Change

Our senses are continually bombarded with various stimuli that become candidates for storage in either our long-term or short-term memory banks. Prior to storage, sensory information passes in the form of electrical impulses first into our short-term bank for immediate use. It stays there for a short while and then will be discarded unless it is rehearsed.

The most familiar example is learning a telephone number just long enough to dial it. However, if you dial it frequently or make an effort to commit it to memory through rehearsal, it goes into your long-term storage bank for recall.

When you practice the exercises in this book, you are rehearsing the information so that it goes into your long-term memory bank. The visual exercises facilitate your associations, which makes it much easier to retrieve the information you have stored away. Imagery is very important to recall.

For example, if you practice visualizing yourself as a sensual, lusty person, that image goes into your long-term memory bank. It stays there waiting for recall. All you have to do is ''ring the bell'' and it's

there at your service. This is why the more you activate your sexual drive, the more it seems to rein-
force itself. If you let sexual images and experiences
fade from your life, eventually your long-term memory bank will discard them—kind of like a house-
keeper getting rid of unused objects. To get them
active again, you will need to rehearse your images
so they go back into your long-term memory bank.

How to Use Erotic Bridges
to Get Sexual Pleasure

What I'm calling transition time is the time it takes in
one's mind to move from a nonerotic state to an erotic
state. I like to think of it as a bridge one crosses from the
"world" of the left brain into the "world" of the right
brain. It's a mental process and is a requirement for good
sex. However, few people ever think about it. Not thinking about it can get you in trouble because, without a
transition time, it becomes more difficult to concentrate
on erotic images and thoughts.

Pleasurable sex is a right-brain activity, an act of the
senses. But many of our daily activities are left-brain activities, acts of our logical mind. Housework, paperwork,
business decisions, and dealing with children mostly require left-brain operations. Rarely do these activities
stimulate our senses in a sensual way.

If we conceptualized the compartments of our brain
as rooms in a house, we can think of having to move
from one room to the next. For easy reference, the right-
brain room will be referred to as RBR and the left-brain
room as LBR. Moving from one room to another takes

time. Yet we often expect ourselves or our partners to move rapidly from left-brain activities into a sexy, amorous place. Alan's situation is an example of someone who initially ignored the need for a transition time.

Alan, a computer analyst, arrived home each night at around 6:30 P.M., after an hour and a half commute on the freeway. Not surprisingly, he was frazzled and liked to sit and read the paper before dinner. After eating he liked to watch a little television to help him relax even further. By 9 P.M. when the kids were in bed, Alan felt very sleepy and usually fell asleep on the couch. Also, not surprisingly, Alan and his wife had little sex in their life.

At the insistence of his wife, Alan joined her in sex therapy. When I first talked to him he expressed hostility at being there. Yes, he also wanted more sex in their life, but he felt tremendous work pressures and he didn't need more pressure in the form of sexual expectations. Wasn't his wife expecting too much for him to be amorous at the end of a very long day? By 9 P.M. he was feeling sleepy, not sexy.

I asked them what sort of things they did to help make a transition from their task-oriented life of work and children to their sensual-oriented life of affection and sexuality. They were both stumped by the question. What did I mean by a transition? In the early part of their relationship they had never had to "force" a transition. They were always turned on then. Alan was convinced the problem was his wife's lack of appreciation for how hard he worked. He didn't think "transitions" had anything to do with it.

Alan was in the situation of being so focused on one issue, he was missing an essential element of the problem. Because of his narrow focus, I knew it would be difficult for Alan to motivate himself at 9 P.M. to try an experiment. His energy level would be low and this would tend to prove his theory. I also knew this could be changed by allowing an appropriate transition time. Anything that would change his energy level would allow Alan to move away from his focus. Something physical, such as a walk, would allow this to happen, but Alan needed to trust this.

At that point, I asked Alan to go on a short visual trip with me. I had him close his eyes and breathe deeply until he was feeling relaxed and comfortable. Then I had him visualize himself getting up from the couch at 9 P.M. and going for a walk with his wife. He was to focus only on the air, sky, breeze, stars, and any other images that aroused his senses. I asked him to imagine that he and his wife were holding hands and talking only about how their senses were being stimulated. There was to be no conversation about the kids, work, in-laws, or other anxiety-producing topics.

Then I had him come back to the room and I asked him how he felt. He said, "Very refreshed." I suggested he try this experiment only once the next week. If he felt unmotivated, he was to repeat the visualization experience while still on the couch.

When they came back the following week, he admitted being pleasantly surprised. It had been very difficult for him to change directions and actually activate himself at a time he was used to winding down. He found the visualization helpful and once he was outside and breathing the night air, he felt refreshed and more energetic than he imagined. He even mentioned feeling a tiny bit sexy.

It makes sense that allowing for transition is a prerequisite to being able to concentrate, no matter what the situation. If your boss or your kids are hassling you and then you're expected to concentrate on making an important decision, your ability to do so will be compromised. If you're in the midst of washing the dishes or reading a book and your partner initiates a sexual overture, your first instinct will be one of "I'm not really in the mood."

If you think about it, why should you be in the mood? Your mind was in your LBR. Some people attempt to proceed anyway, without allowing for a transition. Ninety-nine percent of the time, they will have trouble concentrating on pleasure because they haven't moved to the RBR. If instead of acting on your first instinct, you ask yourself what you could do to make the transition, you'll find that being able to concentrate is much easier.

Women are particularly vulnerable to the problem of transition time. That's because for the majority of women, their home is also their place of work. Even if they work outside the home as well, there are always reminders of how much work is not done. The home is also the place where most sexual activity is supposed to take place, so women are expected to be sexual in their "work" environment. I wonder how many men would tend to feel sexual on the job when surrounded by constant reminders of work left undone?

Because most sexual activity takes place in the home, it makes it more difficult and, therefore, more important that women learn how to make the transition from a nonerotic state to an erotic state. Both they and their partners need to factor transition time and activities into their very busy, left-brain life.

Exercise: Discovering Your Erotic Bridges to Pleasure

Each individual will have unique transition activities that work for them. However, anything that focuses on the senses tends to be effective. It may be a warm bath, a walk outside, a massage, a visual experience such as a video or magazine, or an erotic conversation. Take time right now to make a list of the transition activities that you know work for you. You might find you're stumped at first because you haven't thought about this before. Really give it some thought though, and you'll be surprised. For example, one of my patients discovered that a playful wrestle with her husband really turned her on. Show your list to your partner and have him or her make a list to show you. Or the two of you can do this exercise together.

Are You Having Trouble Concentrating during Sex? Techniques That Help

The mind is the most powerful of all our sex organs. This means, contrary to popular belief, our sexuality is between our ears and not between our legs. Because this is true, our sexuality is extremely vulnerable to values, beliefs, experiences, and imagination. This can be both good and bad. It can be good because positive values, beliefs, experiences, and imagery enhance our sexual capacity. Conversely, their negative counterparts prevent sexual happiness by interfering with concentration.

Good sex requires a blank mind—like a clean slate that can be filled with erotic feelings, images, and sensations. It takes concentration to fill the slate. If our slate is already filled with negative emotions, we won't be able to concentrate on filling it with eroticism.

Most of the time we're not aware of the negative emotions. That's because emotions are abstract. What does an emotion "look" like? How do we know what negative emotion might be blocking our concentration? The visualization exercises in this book will help you associate your negative emotions with images. Then you can do something to change them. Jerry's story is an example of how this is done.

At the age of ten, Jerry and his thirteen-year-old cousin played some sexual games that involved intercourse. These games happened only a few times and eventually faded out. He was never caught and never punished for these games. Yet, as an adult, Jerry became impotent at the moment of intercourse. He says he just stopped feeling pleasurable sensations and simply lost his erection. Up until that point everything felt "just great." Then suddenly, he would lose his ability to stay focused. His mind would wander and the pleasurable sensations would leave him.

Until he sought sex therapy, it never occurred to him that there could be a relationship between his early sex play experiences and his current impotence. He has no memory of ever receiving any negative sexual messages. Yet, his adult conscience was reacting to his violation of a taboo by prohibiting him from enjoying complete sex. Although Jerry couldn't identify his emotion as guilt, he did say he somehow felt that his sexual failures were a "punishment" of some sort.

Here's how Jerry wiped his slate clean. I asked him to do a visualization and to associate an image with the feeling of being punished. The image that came to mind was a giant hypodermic needle that was being stuck in his penis prior to intercourse. This image was so unpleasant that Jerry was eager to mentally destroy the needle. In fact, he had fun thinking about all the ways he could get rid of it. He finally decided he wanted to smash it with a rock. Jerry practiced the image of smashing the needle just prior to intercourse. Soon he found he didn't need the image anymore because he was no longer experiencing impotency.

Janis, a friend not a patient, thought I would appreciate this story. Her situation is another example of how vulnerable eroticism is to negative images. Married three years, she had noticed her ability to be orgasmic dropped dramatically in the last nine months. Once highly arousable, she now found herself wishing it would just "be over with." Her mind would start to think about a telephone call she had to make, a birthday card she needed to buy, or a dress she had to pick up at the cleaners. Her ability to concentrate was suddenly gone. Very much in love with her husband, she didn't understand why she suddenly began to feel so emotionally uninvolved.

It wasn't until she talked this over with a new friend at a weight-loss clinic that she found the connection between her recent twenty extra pounds and her loss of sexuality. Her friend who had successfully lost weight talked about how sexy she was feeling now that she had taken off the pounds.

Until that discussion, Janis simply wasn't aware of her strong association between a sleek, sexy body and the "right" to sexual enjoyment. Before this happened to her, Janis would have said it was crazy to let a few extra pounds ruin your sex life. Janis's new insight didn't take off the weight, but in her case the insight was enough to clear her mental slate.

Loss of concentration can also be related to boredom. Any negative emotion that interferes with sexual concentration could end in sexual boredom. When you can't concentrate, you can't be truly involved. It's the involvement that keeps us from being bored. Have you ever lost interest in someone sexually and been unable to understand why? Here's an example of what one woman did.

Bob and Sue came to therapy with the complaint that there was very little sex in their lives. Both were in their late thirties and they had been married less than three years. They still had fresh memories of the passionate sex that had once been a part of their relationship. Very much in love with each other, they were puzzled by Sue's growing sexual indifference, now beginning to border on aversion.

After several sessions of intense therapeutic investigating, the surprising culprit was finally identified: Shower Power—a power struggle over who went first in the shower. Fortunately for them, *both* Bob and Sue preferred showering before sex. Unfortunately, they did not enjoy sharing the rather small shower that was available to them. That meant someone had to go first. It also meant that the person who went first had to *wait* for the person who went second. Without realizing it, showering first became the less-desirable position.

At Bob's request, Sue initially agreed to the "subordinate" position. Her original acquiescing soon turned into habit. As this situation repeated itself again and again, Sue would lie in bed waiting for Bob to finish his shower. In the beginning, what seems like five minutes began to seem like ten, then twenty. With each episode of waiting, Sue's ability to focus on pleasure was being replaced by unrecognized anger. Red lights began flashing in her mind, stopping the flow of arousal. By the time Bob came to bed, Sue was totally turned off. Sometimes she would participate, but her eroticism was blocked and she stopped being orgasmic, and, eventually, even being aroused. Unable to concentrate on pleasurable feeling, Sue, at first, felt indifferent toward sex. As the months went on, the indifference turned to reluctance and then to avoidance. By the time she came into therapy she was complaining that all she could think about during sex was how much work there was to be done around the house.

When you read about this, it seems impossible that this couple couldn't see what was creating the problem— it seems so obvious. Although it's true that "a rose is sometimes just a rose," it's a mistake to think that human beings operate with much insight into their own personal motivations. When it comes to our own personal life, we frequently can't see the forest for the trees. Once Bob and Sue were able to see the forest, the solution did seem simple: Alternate who showered first.

Getting Back on Track

Have you ever watched a small child at work on a drawing? His or her concentration is usually so intense the child loses all self-consciousness and his or her tongue starts to hang out. As mentioned in chapter 1, this intense concentration is sometimes called a flow state. We all experience flow states. Remember the last time you were so engrossed in something that when the phone rang, it startled you so much that your heart was pounding?

Really great sex occurs when we allow ourselves to enter a concentrated state in which we abandon self-consciousness. Like the child with the tongue hanging out, we need to let it "all hang out." Spectatoring, or watching yourself, interferes with this self-abandonment.

The human mind is an intricate network of pathways or highways leading to and from important control centers. Thoughts are like cars traveling back and forth across the roads. The control centers are like traffic lights, allowing thoughts, instead of cars, to move from one road to the next. During sex, when all systems are "go," all the lights are green and the flow of erotic traffic is smooth. But, if during any point in the sexual experience, your internal jury passes harsh judgment, a red light is turned on and all flow of traffic halts, pleasure is stopped dead in its tracks.

The examples above demonstrate that red lights can come from a multitude of different sources, all acting as distractions that interfere with concentration. Guilt, shame, lack of nurturing touch, body image concerns, power struggles, fears of performance, resentments, and fears of abandonment are all sources of distractions.

I've spent a lot of time talking about what can cause lack of concentration because I believe that in order to get back on track, we have to know what's blocking our way. Remember, good sex requires a clean mental slate. We can't erase the negative images on the slate if we don't know what they are. The chapters that follow will help you identify what some of your blocks might be. The visualizations will help you erase the slate clean, so you can start fresh.

Before you begin your first visualization, however, there are some important guidelines to remember about concentration that will help you stay on track both with the visualizations and during sex.

Concentration Guidelines

- In the beginning, expect some fluctuation in your ability to stay focused
- Don't try to repress or fight any distractions; instead acknowledge them; say, "Hello, distraction. I know you. Now you can go away."

- Let the thoughts pass through you; thoughts generate from the mind, the mind has the power to let them go
- Be patient with yourself; it takes a little time to learn any new task
- Practice; you probably won't get it right the first time; you will get it right, however, if you patiently practice

So, now you're ready to do your first visualization. The purpose of this visualization is to help you remember the concentration guidelines mentioned above. Because this is your first visualization, you might want to review the relaxation techniques listed in chapter 1. Then try the following visualization.

Smoke from a Skywriter

Imagine yourself in a sexual situation in which you're having trouble concentrating on the immediate sensations, feelings, and pleasures. Distracting thoughts keep entering your head, like an old song you can't get out of your mind. Now imagine the thoughts rising out of your mind and settling on white, puffy clouds that are floating above you. Like the smoke from a skywriting plane, the thoughts start to fade and you can no longer read what they are. Eventually they're gone altogether and you're now free to concentrate on the pleasures of the moment.

CHAPTER 3

Getting in Touch with Touching

▼

Over the years, my clients have taught me a very important lesson: *While sex is something, touch is everything.* Touching with a sexual partner is both a sensation and a communication. Think about the different sensation you get from a very gentle touch that may be sensual or a very heavy touch that may be painful. And think about how touch also acts as a communication. For example, if you ask your partner to massage your neck, and he or she does it harshly and quickly, what message do you get? If the sensations aren't pleasurable and the communication positive, then the sex will be unenjoyable.

You can't touch somebody without sending a message at the same time. That's why touch is so important to great sex. Our skin is like a radar screen, picking up even the slightest of nuances. Like other right-brain activities, there is an intuitive component to the sensation of being touched. Through touch we know whether our partner wants to be there, whether they're interested, excited, bored, or indifferent.

You can't take touch for granted if you want great sex in your life. In sex therapy, I often assign couples to do touching "homework" in which they experiment with different kinds of touches on different parts of their bodies and then talk about it with each other. Most couples when they get this assignment respond with the remark,

"This is simple, we do this all the time." However, when I ask them to experiment with both the sensation and communication aspect of their sexual touching, they often find out some surprising information.

For example, Jason and Marissa learned after twenty years of marriage that a certain area around the outside of Marissa's breasts was extremely sensitive to arousal, only if caressed in a certain way, however. Marissa had always thought Jason didn't like stimulating her breasts because his touch seemed so "disinterested," so she felt awkward asking him to try other methods. Jason, on the other hand, didn't think Marissa cared for breast stimulation because she didn't "respond" very much. Their solution had been to leave breast stimulation out of their lovemaking. This new discovery added a whole new dimension to their lovemaking because Marissa found she could more quickly get turned on. This relieved some of the pressure she felt to catch up with Jason, who always seemed to turn on "like a light bulb."

What Sexual Message Does Your Touch Say?

Unlike the simplistic sexual connection animals make, human beings bring complex emotions into their sex lives. Emotions such as jealousy, competition, power, rejection, anger, resentment, and trust (to name only a few) complicate sexuality and can dramatically influence touch. Carolyn and Mike are an example of how lack of trust can influence sexual touch. Married for three years, Carolyn was insisting on sex therapy because Mike so preferred intercourse to foreplay that Carolyn was rarely able to get aroused. Penetration was difficult because she wasn't lubricated. When this happened, Mike would lose his erection. I put a ban on intercourse and asked them to take turns touching one another for twenty minutes each. They were both surprised to learn that Mike could easily spend time touching Carolyn, but was uncomfortable being touched by Carolyn.

Further exploration found that Mike had been raised in a series of foster homes and had never experienced the early bonding between parent and child. Intimate touch didn't seem "real" or trustworthy to him. Unknowingly, he avoided the discomfort of this feeling by avoiding foreplay altogether. Once he discovered the reason for rushing toward intercourse, Mike was willing to spend some therapy time dealing with his "touch aversion" issues. Through brief but repeated exposure to intimate touch from Carolyn, Mike was slowly able to build up trust and not re-create those early feelings of discomfort.

Although Mike's early touch deprivation was extreme, male infants and children receive far less nurturing touch than female children. Consequently, males are more likely to be uncomfortable with intimate touch. If the discomfort is high, men will oversexualize their relationships with woman. Like Mike, the focus will be placed on intercourse as a way to avoid intimate touch. Sometimes these men will have a series of relationships, all very sexual in the beginning, but ending quickly if they feel it's getting too intimate.

Anger and resentment are two other emotions that frequently get in the way of intimate touch. Intimate touch is like giving a gift to your partner. We usually don't feel like giving a gift to an enemy. If you've recently had a fight with your partner, it's easy to acknowledge that you don't feel intimate or sexy. The problem comes in, however, when you're engaged in a low-level but long-standing feud. That's when intimate contact disappears from your relationship and you don't seem to know why. More about this in a later chapter.

Three Kinds of Touch

The above examples (and many others akin to it) have caused me to reflect on the nature of intimate touch and its relationship to long-term, satisfying sex. Intimate touch is really made up of three distinct kinds of touch: nurturing, sensual, and sexual. These three kinds of touch, necessary for a healthy, happy sex life, are all right-brain activities and, fortunately, can be cultivated with practice.

Nurturing Touch

Nurturing touch is that which makes us feel accepted, cared for, and loved. All human beings need nurturing touch. However, this makes us vulnerable to another human being—which can be scary. So sex sometimes becomes a decoy for our nurturing needs. Mike's situation, described above, is one example of how this can interfere with good sex. It doesn't have to be this way. Simply by acknowledging that we mainly meet our nurturing needs through sexual intimacy, we can ensure that this dimension of touch is incorporated into our sexual experiences.

Our first experience with touch is as a newborn and is both formative and crucial to later adult physical intimacy. In the early years of our lives, nurturing touch is essential to survival. An infant that is sheltered and fed but does not receive nurturing touch will fail to develop and grow. This syndrome is called failure to thrive. In its extreme form (never being held or cuddled), a child simply withers away and dies of an inability to absorb nutrients from the food it receives. In its less extreme form (held but not truly loved), a child develops and grows but mistrusts touch. Mike's situation is an example of this.

As adults, in order to both give and receive nurturing touch we must have had it as an infant and child. Nurturing touch, like most other human behaviors, is learned. Without experiencing it, we don't incorporate giving or receiving it into our repertoire of behaviors. For some, this can be a void that creates severe emotional pain. Consider, for example, the following story.

Lucy contacted me several months after she had been to see a woman doctor for an athletic injury she had experienced. Lucy was very frightened about her preoccupation with this doctor. Married for five years, Lucy felt content and still very much in love with her husband. Why should she be thinking about this woman doctor all the time? Lucy felt certain she wasn't gay, but she was fearful of the strong attraction and the way in which it made her feel distant from her husband. I asked her to think back on any other time in her life when she felt like this and she could remember two other times when she was preoccupied by thoughts of another woman.

In the second grade, Lucy had a woman teacher who took a strong liking to her. Lucy remembers her as loving, gentle, understanding, and affectionate. She very much recalls wishing this woman was her mother. Later, in junior high, she had a gym teacher whom she also greatly admired and who gave Lucy encouragement and compliments. She felt as if she had a crush on this woman, but it didn't feel sexual at all.

Now, at age thirty, Lucy was once again feeling like she had a crush on a woman. Like the other two experiences, this one didn't feel sexual either but, still, Lucy was worried. Was she possibly a closet homosexual and not being honest with herself? To answer this I had to know more about Lucy's background, especially with nurturing touch.

Lucy's early experiences with touch were typical of

home life with an alcoholic. Her father, an angry drunk, dominated the household. Lucy, her two older brothers, and her mother spent most of their time trying to stay out of his way. Lucy remembers her mother as being timid and frightened. She has no memory of ever being held, cuddled, reassured, or comforted by any family member.

It's not strange that a seven year old who had never experienced nurturing touch would overidentify with the first woman who was really loving toward her—her second-grade teacher. Lucy *was* looking for a substitute caring mother. Her fantasy, projected onto her teacher, preoccupied her until she was forced by circumstances to move on. Later, in junior high, the same situation was re-created by a woman who was caring toward Lucy. Now, at age thirty, her encounter with a sympathetic, understanding female physician was re-creating her childhood and adolescent fantasy, thus, the preoccupation.

What Lucy needed now in order to heal the old hurts was some experience with nurturing touch. To turn the fantasy into a reality, she needed to both give and receive nurturing touch. What she did was to volunteer to work on the pediatric ward of her local hospital. This was an environment in which nurturing was desperately needed and in which the children were appreciative in return. After some months the thoughts of the female doctor disappeared and were replaced, for the first time ever, with thoughts about becoming a mother. Until this point, Lucy had felt she could never nurture a child.

Her relationship with her husband changed as well. They began attending Adult Children of Alcoholics (ACA) meetings together and took some classes on communication in marriage. Lucy was feeling a growing intimacy with her husband and began to realize that this was the void that had been causing the burning pain inside her for so long. The sex, which had seemed so mechanical before, now seemed more loving and mutual.

Lucy's and Mike's situations demonstrate how missing out on early nurturing touch can effect adult sexuality. Unfortunately, this "nurturing neglect" is more common than we realize. And recently we've become aware that there is a situation more severe than neglect that profoundly impacts on adult sexuality—child sexual molestation. The impact of early abuse on the ability to enjoy adult sexuality takes a variety of forms. My experience with using visualization to "undo" some of the damage done by abuse has been quite remarkable.

Peter was a patient in one of my sexual abuse visualization groups. As a result of his repeated sexual abuse, he felt his body was vile. After all, if his body was used in such a harmful way, it must be something about which he should be terribly ashamed. Feeling undeserving of nurturing touch, he chose instead to overeat. In Peter's unconscious mind, this gave his undeserving feelings some legitimacy. Without realizing it, Peter was giving women an "excuse" not to touch his offensive body.

In the group, we worked with images of his body as a beautiful Greek statue, admired and appreciated for its aesthetic value. With practice, Peter began to "see" that his previous images were inventions of his mind and thus could be replaced with healthier images, also inventions of his mind. By the end of the group, Peter was ready to take better care of his body and finally felt deserving of a good woman. He had even developed a list of qualities in a woman that would affirm him as a person. For the first time in his life, he felt optimistic that he could enjoy the *nurturing* touch of a loving woman. He no longer needed to eat to keep them away.

Bonnie, also a member of the group, had a different problem she was working on. Her abuse had left her with a strong connection between physical touching and physical pain. When she attempted intercourse with her husband, she could feel her body go numb. It was a "trick" she had learned as an infant in order to cope with her abuse. "You can't feel the pain if you can't feel anything," her young mind reasoned.

Bonnie's visualizations consisted of a woven rope. She saw two parts of the rope, one being pain, the other pleasure. In her visualization, she worked with unraveling the rope to separate pain from pleasure. In this way, she began to see that touching did not always bring pain and she would not have to go numb to avoid having the pain. She began to let go of the need to numb her body and to allow her body to experience pleasure.

If you're having real problems with receiving and giving nurturing touch or you have been a victim of abuse, sexual or physical, you need to consult professional help to resolve these issues. The last chapter of this book discusses how to select a therapist and how to use visualizations with the therapist you do select.

The following visualization will help you to recall some nurturing opportunities from birth to present. The point is you get a "second chance" by reliving these opportunities through visualization. This can be very healing if you missed out the first time around. If it seems like make-believe, remember that our mind creates our images and can, therefore, change those images. Bonnie's situation is an example of this.

* * *

▼

Elevator Descent

Imagine yourself on an elevator at the top floor of a tall building. The number of the top floor is equivalent to your current age. Slowly let the elevator descend toward the bottom as you watch the floor numbers decrease. With each descent in floor, you are returning to a prior year in your life. When you get to the ground floor, you're back in your infancy. Imagine yourself being held, cuddled, and spoken to very tenderly by a loving person. Let yourself feel the love and the tenderness that you are being given. Feel the safety and security that comes from knowing you are loved. Experience the gentleness and caring of the touch. Enjoy the sensations and feelings of being nurtured.

Now get back on the elevator and go up a few floors until you are three years of age. Imagine yourself outside playing. You fall down and hurt yourself and run crying to an adult who takes you in his or her arms and comforts you. The adult's strong, loving touch reassures you that everything will be all right. The world feels safe again and you are ready to go back to playing.

Get back on the elevator and go to the fifth floor. You're five years old and your parents have left you at a relative's house for the night. You climb into a strange bed to go to sleep and suddenly feel very afraid of everything that is so unfamiliar. You reach out for your favorite cuddly object that you brought with you and hold it close to you. As you stroke it rhythmically and smell its familiar smell, you begin to feel safe. Being able to hold and touch something so familiar gives you great comfort. The physical closeness soothes away your fears and soon you drift into a dreamy slumber.

Get back on the elevator and go to the top floor. When you get off, you're at your current age. Imagine yourself with an important person in your life that you know to be nurturing. See yourself being tenderly held, stroked, and caressed in a loving and caring way. Let yourself feel the security and comfort being touched gives to you. Surrender to the feeling of the person's power to make you feel safe with his or her nurturing touch.

▲

Sensual Touch

The main purpose of sensual touch is also nonerotic pleasure. Sensual touch stimulates and heightens all of our senses. Unfortunately, too many of us are programmed to think only in terms of sex when we think of sensuality. We shortchange ourselves by such narrow thinking. Stroking a cat or dog, licking whipped cream off your fingers, rustling a child's hair, and rubbing your face with a warm towel after a shower are all examples of sensual touch that is not sexual. In each of these situations, your senses are being stimulated in a pleasurable way. If we're not open to that kind of stimulation, we don't get the benefits. Learning to expand our definition of sensuality will amplify the pleasures life has to offer. It will also help you move into your right brain during sex where much ecstasy awaits you.

Although nurturing touch is necessary for our mental and physical well-being, sensual touch exists on a higher plane. We can live without sensual touch—but our life would be deprived of simple, free pleasures. Just as we can live without ever experiencing a spectacular sunset, we can survive without cultivating our sensuality.

But just as the quality of our life is immeasurably heightened by such a spectacle of nature, so our life is enhanced by the experience of sensuality. And ultimately, a sensually aware person is a sexually attractive partner.

Our need for sensual touch is too often forced to go underground and hide out like a fugitive. As in the case with nurturing touch, there is little cultural recognition of the human need for sensual touch. Because we are taught to consciously ignore this need, we rush through those activities that could allow us much pleasure: Showers are quick and purposeful, back rubs merely eliminate soreness or pain, nails are painted for appearance, handshakes are introductory and brief, whirlpools remain unused, and sex is quick and orgasmically oriented. In short, we're a culture oriented toward purpose over pleasure: left brain over right once again.

Exercise: Heightening Your Senses

A very simple exercise you can do each day to help activate your right brain is to make a mental list each morning before you get out of bed. It takes less than a minute to think about what sensual pleasures you might experience that day. Decide in your mind, what sensual pleasure you want to highlight for the day. For example, instead of quickly washing your hair, take time to concentrate on the various sensations you can get from the experience. If you do it slowly and sensuously, you'll get a different feeling than if you do it brusquely. The more you pay attention to the sensations, the more nurtured you'll feel throughout the day. And by picking a new activity each day and focusing on its sensuality, you will be surprised at how heightened your senses will become. If you're suspect to the possibilities of the benefit of such an exercise, consider how acute the hearing is of someone who is blind.

This exercise is important to you because by heightening your senses you will become a more sensually aware person, a more right-brain person. You will be doing it without having to use stimulants such as alcohol or drugs. Your sexual pleasure will take on a new dimension of sensuality that will, in turn, increasingly arouse your sexual partner's senses. It's paying attention to these very simple, everyday activities that offer you the opportunity to enhance your right brain that make the difference between exciting, involved sex and sexual indifference or boredom.

The following visualization will enhance your awareness of sensual touching.

Sensual Ecstasy

Imagine yourself alone, walking in a lovely meadow filled with wildflowers. The air around you is clear, fresh, and sweet with the smell of wildflowers. The sun is out and you can feel its warmth as it surrounds you like a comforting blanket. The sky is blue and filled with soft, puffy clouds that make you feel light as a feather. Birds are singing a melodic song.

You're feeling so light your feet are slightly lifted off the ground and your body is slowly becoming horizontal so that you are on your back, floating on a bed of wildflowers. You feel relaxed, supported, safe, and dreamy. Someone you really like and trust approaches you and sits down behind you so your head is resting very lightly in his or her lap. The person begins caressing your face with his or her hands; the touch is firm but gentle. As the person massages your temples, your body relaxes even more. Your attention drifts back and forth between the wonderful feeling of the touch and the stimulation of your other senses: the sweet smell of the flowers, the pleasantly warm sun on your body, the soft breeze as it calmly brushes against you, and the musical sounds of the birds. All of your senses are being stimulated and you're experiencing a sensual ecstasy.

Now that you've enhanced your sensual awareness, here's a visualization that will help you communicate to your partner the places on your body that are most sensual.

* * *

The Anatomy Chart

Imagine yourself in front of a large anatomy chart of your body. Your lover is your student and you are proudly telling him or her about your body, which you know intimately. He or she is fascinated by you and eager to learn what you have to say. With a pointer you indicate to him or her the parts of your body that respond most pleasurably to his or her touch. You tell your lover exactly where and how he or she can give your body the greatest pleasure.

Sexual Touching

This kind of touch *is specifically oriented toward physiological arousal of the genitals.* It's not touch that is limited to the genitals, but includes any kind of touch on any part of the body that arouses. Because nature endowed our bodies with a pleasurable response to sexual touch, we all have the capacity to enjoy it. It's an exquisite gift, but it comes with conditions and, therefore, should never be taken for granted. In order to experience the pleasure, we must be relaxed and able to remain in our right brain, where pleasure originates.

The ability to enjoy sexual touch is fragile. Many things can interfere, causing us to temporarily lose this gift. Using sex to prove masculinity, femininity, power, or control will rob us of the gift. Expectations to perform instead of enjoy will steal pleasure away from us. Negative images that create feelings of shame, guilt, or fear will pillage the gift. The key is to remain in our right brain and let nature's gift take over.

The following visualization will help you to enjoy sexual touch.

Erotic Zones

Imagine yourself somewhere in a secluded and private spot. It may be a mountain cabin, a beach home on a cliff, or some other place your mind takes you. Perhaps there is a fire going, a breathtaking view, and a comfortable bed, couch, rug, or all three. The important thing is that your environment feels comfortable, safe, and private. Music may be playing in the background.

Now turn your creative attention to having another person with you. On the canvas of your mind, paint exactly what this person would be like. Then let this person come alive and be with you.

Visualize that you are being touched in erotic ways. The parts of your body that are most sensitive are being touched. Fingers, toes, ears, buttocks, genitals, nipples, breasts, or any other erotic zone can be included. Think about how you like to be touched and imagine that touch. As you keep this scene in mind, you'll notice your body beginning to tingle and you feel a pleasant sensation in your genitals. There is a slight restlessness in your body and a desire to move your pelvis. The arousal feels exciting but without a need to do anything more than enjoy the pleasure of the feeling.

The Total Touch—
What It Can Do for Your Sex Life

When sexual touch coexists with both nurturing and sensual touch, really great sex occurs. The fusing of the three make up the Total Touch or Intimate Touch. It's the package deal—the combination—that makes for long-term, satisfying sex. Nurturing and sensual touch can easily exist on their own; they're valuable in their own right. But, anyone who has experienced sexual touch in the absence of its two counterparts, knows it can feel mechanical, ritualistic, and unconnected.

I am reminded of the informal survey Ann Landers took of her female readers several years back. Would they choose being held and cuddled over the "act" of sex? Given this either/or situation, the overwhelming response was a choice for nurturing. The results of the survey caused quite a stir. The uproar came because the results were interpreted to indicate that women don't care about sexual intercourse. Nothing could be further from the truth.

What a survey worded in this way couldn't really tell us is that women care a great deal about intercourse, but not in the absence of nurturing and sensuality. Being wise, they want the whole package. And they're not alone. Forced to answer the same question a male's cultural teaching would pressure him to select "the act" over being cuddled, lest he be labeled a wimp. In reality, there are few men who derive pleasure from sexual intercourse that is severed from nurturing and sensuality. However, in our culture, only the very brave and the very honest man would admit to it.

Remember Carolyn and Mike, the couple who were having difficulty because Mike would rush to have intercourse to avoid intimate touching? Mike was disbelieving at first, but once he learned to trust touch, he and Carolyn went onto a new level of sexual joy. Instead of almost no foreplay, they found themselves sometimes spending an hour or more enjoying all three kinds of touch. Their newfound total touch was like a new toy to them. Mike admitted that he had changed so much it was becoming very difficult for him to listen to other men "sexualize" women. He used to enjoy drinking with his buddies and making sexual comments about every woman who came into the room. Now, because he thought of sex as so much more than intercourse, he felt his buddies' comments showed little insight into the expansiveness of sex. He thought his newfound sexual joy was worth the trade-off for the evening with his buddies.

The Total Touch Relieves Sexual Boredom

Early in our new love relationships, passion is intense and powerful. Often, the passion makes it seem easy to give nurturing and sensual touch along with sexual touch. Unfortunately, in the maturing process of our relationships, nurturing and sensual touch slowly evaporate and sexual touch is left to stand on its own. In many of the chapters, you will discover why we all have a tendency to let the nurturing and sensuality slip away from our relationships. After years of being together, intimate touching takes on a perfunctory quality, as exemplified by the ritualistic hello or goodbye kiss that takes place in many of our long-term relationships.

On its own, sexual touch creates a calculated, what's-in-it-for-me climate. Feelings of being used start to appear and we start to pull back from each other. The long, relaxed, and passionate sexual sessions become, over time, to feel like work instead of enjoyment. Within these parameters, the overall quality of our sex takes on a lack of true involvement. You'll remember reading in chapter 1 that the lack of involvement is the central issue in feeling bored. So it naturally flows that sex becomes boring when we are left with only sexual touch.

Jack and Kelly are representative of many of the couples I see who seek sex therapy because they are unhappy with the frequency of their sex. They've been married for about four years now and it's the first marriage for both. They are thinking about having children but want to straighten out what they feel are serious sexual problems in the marriage before they make such a long-term commitment.

Both Jack and Kelly expressed an overall lack of enthusiasm for sexual encounters. Sometimes they would think about it during the day and would plan in their mind to approach their partner that night. However, it rarely seemed to happen. The good intentions were replaced by preoccupation with other tasks that needed to be done or simply by watching television. When they did get together on occasion, the sex was good; this confused them even more.

When asked about what sort of issues they argued about, they both agreed that although they argued about a few unimportant matters, on the whole they thought they had a pretty good marriage. In their mind, sex was the only problem. Both were puzzled about the infrequency of the sex, because they felt their commitment to each other was as strong now as when they decided to marry. When I inquired further about the "unimportant" issues they argued about, they both laughed and said it was silly and certainly not something that should interfere with sex.

As I asked them to explain what issues they did argue about, Jack and Kelly became defensive. Kelly wanted Jack to do more around the house because she had a full-time job outside the house. She didn't think she was asking too much of him. Jack said he did more than most men he knew and he thought that if Kelly would do a better job of picking up after herself there wouldn't be so much clutter to put away.

What accompanied their defensiveness was a change in body language. Kelly and Jack slightly turned their bodies away from each other and I could sense a pulling away that frequently occurs during couples' disagreements. It became obvious to me that their attempt to minimize this issue was having a serious impact on their physical contact with each other. The tendency for couples to minimize the specifics is something I frequently see as a therapist. You may think you are arguing about toothpaste tops, watching television, late-night snacking, or other nonserious issues, but what you may not realize is that, although the specifics may be irrelevant what they symbolize is crucial to harmony. What the ''little things'' symbolized to Kelly and Jack was unknowingly a struggle for power.

As so frequently happens with us, the intimate quality of touching is destroyed by a competitive, right or wrong tug-of-war. Research on couples' relationships indicate that the single most destructive aspect of a relationship is a power struggle. Just like Bob and Sue (described in chapter 2), Kelly and Jack were mired down in an unspoken contest to see who was going to get their way. However insidious and disguised, the loving relationship was being usurped by an adversarial relationship. Former friends were becoming undeclared enemies; instinctively, we avoid intimacy with our enemy.

I asked each of them to take time over the next week to spend a few minutes visualizing their early lovemaking sessions and then their more recent sessions. They were to write down a comparison of the two and focus on what they thought were the main differences. I also asked them to spend about forty minutes once that week just touching each other in nonerotic but nurturing and sensual ways. They weren't sure about the writing assignment but they thought the touching session would be easy—it was sex that was the problem, not the touching.

In fact, they didn't do either of the "homework" assignments. After providing me with a list of excuses about how busy they were that week, we began to talk about touching. I asked them to stand up and give each other a hug. Expressing reluctance because they would feel silly, they finally stood up and briefly gave each other an "A-frame" hug; their bodies came together only at the top, leaving a slight distance between the lower parts. Pointing this out to them led to further discussions about touch. Some insights into their difficulty were beginning to emerge. Perhaps touching wasn't as easy as they originally thought. They were reassigned the homework from the previous week.

This time the writing assignments were done, but again the touching session was left undone. After spending time thinking and writing about how their sexual sessions had changed, both Jack and Kelly admitted that they didn't feel like touching each other. They both agreed that what was missing was the pleasure they had felt in giving to the other person. As each held back from fully giving, the sex became more oriented toward orgasm and less toward sensuality and nurturing. The orgasms "fooled" them into believing that their sex was good.

It's certainly not unusual for us to define good sex as mutually satisfying orgasms. Kelly and Jack were just going along with the cultural norm: Good sex equals intercourse plus orgasm. Until our discussions, it hadn't occurred to them that they both wanted more from sex than orgasms. Because they were no longer feeling comfortable giving pleasure, they were both missing out on receiving the extras that sex has to offer. Sex began to feel like a power struggle; each unconsciously wanting the other to give a little more. Even though they were skilled at the mechanics of achieving orgasm, they felt a void in the areas of nurturing and sensual touch. Without these two qualities, lack of involvement set in and boredom soon followed. Of course, avoidance of sex trailed behind.

The solution for Jack and Kelly was twofold: (1) recognizing the importance of their differences so they could openly deal with them and (2) putting the nurturing and sensual touch back into their sex. Because negative emotions easily get in the way of intimate touch, dealing with the conflict is a prerequisite.

If you're feeling that your sexual relationship doesn't contain the total touch here's an exercise that will help you and your partner to get back on course.

Exercise: Your Sexual Shopping List

Imagine you and your partner in a sexual situation. Start at the very beginning and imagine the most typical way in which you get started. In detail, let your mind go through an entire sexual scenario, thinking about the three kinds of touch. Replay the scene several times until you are very familiar with it. Then make a three-column list. The first column is the touching you would like to keep, the second column the touching you would like to discard, and the third column is your "shopping list," the missing touching you want to add. After each of you have made your lists, share them with each other.

CHAPTER 4

How Masturbation Can Improve Partner Sex

▼

It makes sense that intimate touch between partners is an essential ingredient in great sex. But masturbation is touching yourself, what's that got to do with great partner sex? Isn't masturbation really something you do when you don't have a partner? And how is masturbation related to the right-brain idea?

To answer these questions, you have to be willing to leave behind some very strong cultural taboos and to expand your definition of masturbation. When you do, you'll find yourself operating more in your right brain, the place where sexual happiness is stored.

Are Your Notions about Masturbation Part of the Problem or Part of the Solution?

The stroking, caressing, and touching of genitals is natural human behavior, existing in all cultures throughout history. In some cultures, the stroking and caressing of an infant's genitals by an adult is the accepted way of soothing an upset infant. Early childhood experimentation with self-stimulation is a normal progression in the development of sexuality. Like crawling before walking, childhood masturbation is a preparatory stage to adult partner sex.

Yet, no matter how normal and natural masturbation is, it is rare to find an adult who does not blush at the mention of the word. A recent long-distance phone conversation between a friend and me is a case in point:

"So, Carol, how's the book writing going?"
"Pretty good."
"What are you writing on now?"
"You don't want to know."
"Yes, I do."
"No, you don't."
"Yes, I do."
"Masturbation."
"You're right, I don't."

Although I couldn't see his red face over the phone, I knew it was there just the same.

The origin of our embarrassment is very old, rooted in early religion where wasting of seed (semen) was (and, in some cases, still is) condemned as sinful. Much later, in the eighteenth century, wasting semen, in addition to being sinful, was proclaimed to be the cause of mental illness. The association of masturbation with sin and insanity still influences our current beliefs.

Our negative feelings and limited views of masturbation run very deep and, therefore, keep us in our left brain where our inhibitions lie. These negative views have been passed on through centuries of cultural norms, values, and expectations. It's never easy to repudiate cultural imperatives. What we learn from our culture we accept as truth; a truth that is oftentimes out of our awareness.

For example, our parents' generation truly believed that masturbation could cause warts, mental illness, and other terrible defects. We know that isn't true today, but for many a discomfort with masturbation remains because of its past associations. Visualization is a wonderful tool to help us change beliefs and behaviors and more into our right brain. A story from a colleague illustrates this very well.

My friend, also a sex therapist, was telling me about a conversation he had with his fifteen-year-old daughter about masturbation. Feeling strongly about the need to be open and honest with her about sexual matters, he was telling her that masturbation was a very common experience for all age groups. He was extolling the various values when she suddenly, but innocently, asked him, "So, dad, how often do you masturbate?" He could feel his face flush as his impersonal dissertation became unexpectedly very personal. He realized he was almost choking on his words as he finally was able to say, "Well, it varies, depending on circumstances." Admittedly, an evasive and impersonal response directly from his analytical left brain. Even he was surprised at his remarks in light of his "liberal" approach to sexuality.

Because visualization is useful in helping us deal with powerful cultural hand-me-downs that no longer serve a purpose, I suggested to my colleague that he mentally practice this scene with his daughter, this time giving her a more personal response. Several months later he called me to tell me he had braved the subject again and his mental rehearsal had considerably reduced his embarrassment. He was able to tell her that he usually masturbated at least weekly and sometimes more.

Recent sexual surveys indicate a wide variety of behaviors, patterns, and beliefs concerning masturbation. According to the surveys, the majority of us have tried masturbation at one time or another. Men are more likely to masturbate than women, although the number of women who do it continues to steadily increase. A few of us still think it's disgusting and sinful. Conversely, a few of us think it's the greatest thing since sliced bread. Many of us think it's okay as long as there is no available partner. The only common thread in all our beliefs and behaviors is secrecy. Where masturbation is concerned, mum's the word.

The legacy of secrecy and embarrassment about masturbation acts as a censor to your sexual thoughts and feelings, inhibiting your *full* sexual enjoyment. By working with visualizations, you can slowly get rid of this censor and experience acceptance of all parts of your sexuality, including the part that can feel sexual joy from being just with you.

A Historical Look at Masturbation

Because it is such natural behavior, how is it that we've come to be so embarrassed by even the mention of masturbation? The origin of our embarrassment is rooted in early religion, but then fertilized and firmly implanted by an eighteenth-century Swiss physician named Simon André Tissot. Tissot's search for an explanation of the puzzling diseases of his time led him to his theory of sexual degeneracy. At that time in history, before the discovery of germ theory, the cause of disease remained a mystery. Mental illness was especially puzzling. To Tissot, the unusual or unexplainable behavior of mental illness "looked" similar to that of devirilized males, all of which he lumped into the category of degeneracy; a degenerate being a bad, evil, or morally corrupt person.

Because of Tissot's diligent efforts, his theory became accepted in the medical world. In a book written in 1758, he convinced the medical thinkers of his time that the waste of the vital fluid semen was responsible for both physical and mental disease.

He reached his conclusion through a process of deductive thinking involving castration. He observed, as did his predecessors, that one of the effects of castration is the drying up of semen. Thus, wasting semen must cause the devirilizing effects seen in castration. Tissot knew nothing of testosterone, the male hormone, and, therefore, erroneously made his infamous conclusion that masturbation wasthe cause of degeneracy. This conclusion was so powerful that even two centuries later and despite scientific proof otherwise, the mention of the word *masturbation* still gives rise to a rush of facial color.

Tissot's theory, originally in Latin, was not translated into English until 1832. Events in America at that time helped the acceptance of Tissot's claims. Reverend Sylvester Graham, an outspoken follower of Tissot, believed that diet, fitness, and abstinence would defend against the evil temptation of masturbation. Accordingly, he developed a health cracker that supposedly reduced carnal need (appropriately named the graham cracker).

Graham's most devoted and well-known follower was John Harvey Kellogg. Kellogg, a physician, headed the Battle Creek Sanitarium where he incorporated a healthy diet into his treatment of insanity. He processed cereals and nuts and maintained that their substitution for meats would reduce desires of the flesh.

Kellogg was fanatical in his thinking. John Money, in his book *Lovemaps* (1986), writes of Kellogg:

Kellogg was degeneracy theory's most ardent antimasturbation advocate. For intractable cases of masturbation in boys he recommended sewing up the foreskin with silver wire; or, if that failed, circumcision without anesthesia. For girls, he recommended burning out the clitoris with carbolic acid. For fathers, he wrote detailed instructions of how they would silently encroach upon their sleeping sons and rapidly pull back the blankets. An erect penis was prima facie evidence of the sleeping sinner caught in secret vice.

The germ theory of disease and the new science of bacteriology founded by Louis Pasteur and Robert Koch in the 1870s was rejected by Kellogg. Kellogg was so entrenched in his thinking that he saved his semen by sleeping alone and never consummating his marriage (Money 1986).

None of the forefathers of antimasturbation addressed themselves to the issue of sexism in their thinking. Degeneracy theory was based on observations in males but applied to all carnal thoughts, male or female. Exactly how the semen theory applied to women was not explained and neither medicine nor society ever questioned it.

Although most twentieth-century scientists easily left behind the antiquated thinking of Tissot, Graham, and Kellogg, much of society did not. Religion, law, the media, education, and some areas of medicine carried on the association of degeneracy and masturbation. Despite scientific evidence proving otherwise, the long-held beliefs did not easily disappear.

Sexual Self-Discovery— How It Solves the Sexual Doldrums

Most of you think of masturbation as a way to have an orgasm without a partner. It is, of course. But there are other benefits of masturbation that get overlooked. Namely, sexual self-discovery and self-love.

Sexual Self-Discovery

Our early experimentation with self-stimulation acts as a first-step process in the discovery of our sexual self. As children, we are naturally curious about everything in our world. Our bodies are no exception; our exploration takes in all body parts. In the process of touching, we discover the pleasure that comes from our bodies. The pleasure acts as a reinforcement and we naturally gravitate toward touching that results in pleasurable feelings.

This early self-exploration in body pleasures is important for our future sexual relationships. Through this process, we learn to feel good about our bodies. This contributes to the development of a positive body image so essential to satisfying partner sex. When we feel good about our bodies, we are less distracted during sex and more able to move into our right brains so that we can enjoy the pleasure of the experience. Remember the story in chapter 2 of the woman who gained twenty pounds and lost her ability to concentrate? Once she became self-conscious of her body, she was no longer able to fully participate in sex.

Paul is an example of just how important sexual self-discovery can be to partner sex. His story also demonstrates how vulnerable sexuality is to negative emotions such as shame. Paul is single and thirty years old. He came to therapy because he had not dated in six years and was feeling the growing isolation that he himself described as a "security blanket" that he was using to avoid feeling threatened.

Paul's only dating experience occurred in his early twenties when he had two very short-term relationships. Both had ended, according to him, because of sexual problems. He said his fear of repeating the humiliating sexual episodes kept him from even talking to women. In both relationships, he found that he was unable to let the women touch his penis. To him it was more than a reluctance; it felt almost phobic.

With the first woman, he experienced anxiety only after they had removed their clothes and were beginning to make love. Because this was Paul's first experience with sex, he expected some nervousness. He knew, however, something was seriously wrong when the anxiety went sky-high as she began caressing his penis. He was unable to continue and had to put his clothes on and leave the room. This scene repeated itself the next few times they tried to be sexual and, not unexpectedly, the woman refused to see him again.

A year later, Paul met another woman that he dated for a while. This time the anxiety would emerge as soon as he even thought about being naked in front of her. Several months went by and finally the woman began to make sexual overtures toward Paul. He stopped calling her. Six years later he was in my office, having never even talked to another woman on a social basis.

Paul denied any unusual or particularly negative early sexual experiences. He also denied ever masturbating. He thought his childhood was a happy one in which he felt loved. He didn't know why he was so anxious about being touched. He thought it was natural for men and women to want to touch each other and that sex would be a wonderful experience, not the monster it seemed to be for him.

Together, we explored his past in detail, especially any memories about early experimentation with masturbation. He repeatedly denied having any experience with masturbation, negative or positive. He seemed to remember very little about any exposure to sexuality. He said he was extremely shy during his teenage years and had never dated. I asked him if he was willing to try hypnosis to determine if there was some memory he was blocking. He agreed.

Hypnosis is a very deep state of relaxation in which extraneous stimuli are ignored and the mind is able to focus intently on the task at hand. In this relaxed state, the unconscious becomes more accessible. We had several introductory sessions to acquaint Paul with the feeling of deep relaxation and to get him to trust the fact that he would not be out of control—a fear for most people. While under hypnosis, I asked Paul to visualize that first sexual experience he had with the woman he was dating. I asked him to focus in on his exact emotional state at the time and to let himself experience that same emotion now. Then I asked Paul to go back further in time, before the experience with the woman, and recall a previous time in which he felt the exact same emotion. What came to mind surprised Paul.

An image flashed in his mind of being thirteen years old and having a friend over to spend the night. It was late at night and they were in his room. His friend started talking to him about "jerking off" and asked Paul if he had ever tried it. When Paul said no, his friend began to tease him into trying. The friend began demonstrating on himself how to do it. Paul tried to do what his friend was doing, but he felt an ominous feeling that what he was doing was wrong. His friend ejaculated and Paul was mortified.

After the hypnosis, Paul and I talked about his experience. He could then remember how awful it was. At the time he didn't understand why he felt so terrible—only that he did. Paul was finally able to talk about the conflict he felt back then. There was a deep feeling of shame but also a feeling of great excitement at the pleasure he felt touching himself. The two opposing emotions were too much for Paul to deal with. He blocked the experience from his memory.

Although the event was out of his awareness, the experience dealt Paul a serious blow just the same. Any possibility of emerging sexuality threatened to bring back the conflict. Without realizing it, Paul made an unconscious decision to avoid confrontation with the conflict, thus he never dated and never risked being sexual with a partner. He even avoided dealing with his own sexuality by never trying masturbation again. In his twenties, his intellect told him he needed to be more "normal." He tried dating and even tried sex. But years of repressing the conflict caused an explosive reaction—touching his penis was like pushing the button on the explosives.

Paul's case is an extreme example of how a normal process can get off course. If Paul had had the normal, progressive experience with early masturbation and self-discovery, he would not have suddenly been in such an overwhelming place.

Keeping in mind the strategies for change I talked about in chapter 1, what Paul needed now was to go back and experience the sexual self-discovery one step at a time. Like a new skier starts on the bunny slope, Paul needed to start with just learning to touch himself. Prior to any self-touching, Paul and I worked with visualization to reduce his anxiety and lower his resistance. His mental rehearsal slowly gave him confidence while allowing him to deal with the emerging conflict at his own pace. Progress was slow because Paul had been severely damaged. It took over a year for Paul to get comfortable with masturbation. It took another six months for him to ask a girl out on a date. By then Paul was a consummate visualizer and he used visualization to help him manage the anxiety of his first sexual experience. Slowly, with repeated experiences, Paul's phobic reaction disappeared and he was able to have normal sex.

Few of us have experienced the trauma that Paul did. Yet, many of us have been made to feel guilty about sexual self-discovery. In varying ways and amounts, this guilt has prevented us from feeling totally comfortable with our bodies. The bright side is that it's never too late to turn this around by discovering yourself and the many sexual benefits that come from being comfortable with self-stimulation.

David is someone who used his comfort with masturbation to solve his sexual problem with his partner. David was forty when I first met him. He came into therapy shortly after his divorce from his first wife; he had been married for thirteen years. David had very little sexual experience prior to his marriage and married a woman who also was very inexperienced. They were both inhibited, and their sex lacked experimentation and communication. Soon they seemed to lose interest and the frequency of sex dropped to zero. Because of many other problems with the marriage, they chose not to do anything about the lack of sex. For the last five years of their marriage they were totally celibate.

Now David was single again and was ready to leave behind some of his sexual inhibitions. He came to therapy because he was having trouble getting erections with the woman he was dating. I asked David if he had trouble with erections during masturbation. Surprisingly, he answered in rather a proud way that masturbation always "worked" for him. David had been masturbating since he was twelve years old. To him it seemed a natural and normal thing to do—even more than partner sex, which to him seemed more ''complicated.''

We talked about how David might use his comfort with self-stimulation to improve partner sex. I asked him if he thought he might be able to give himself an erection while with his girlfriend. This had not occurred to him because he had always thought of masturbation as a way to have an orgasm when not with a partner. He was intrigued by the idea and was looking forward to giving it a try. When he returned next week he was in high spirits. It had worked. He knew he had broken through some important barriers and his confidence was definitively ''up.'' Relying on his ''old standby'' had allowed him to concentrate on sensations and pleasure rather than monitoring whether he was getting hard. Within a month, David felt much better about his performance during partner sex. Self-stimulation was no longer a necessity but rather an option he could use when he felt like it.

Masturbation is a way to appreciate and know your own body and the pleasurable sensations it can give you. Knowing your own body allows you to be the best lover you can be. If you think you already know everything you need to know about your body, think again. Otherwise, you'll remain stagnant as a lover, never expanding the possible dimensions of your sexual self. The following visualization will be useful in helping you to discover more about your own body.

* * *

The Geiger Counter

Imagine yourself in a private, comfortable, warm room. You feel relaxed, safe, and pleasantly excited about what is ahead. You're naked, lying down on a soft comforter and you're touching your body. You feel naturally curious as to how each part of your body is going to respond to your touch. Your skin contains millions of tiny sensors that give off a pleasant signal when touched. Like a Geiger counter, the more pleasure, the stronger the signal. You're experimenting with different touches and pressures in different places, noticing the difference in signals.

Your genital area is definitely giving off the most significant signal. As you explore the various parts of your genitals, you get signals telling you which part feels the best to a particular kind of touch. When you find the part of your genitals that give you the most pleasure and the loudest signal, you increase the speed of your touch until it reaches a crescendo of pleasure.

The Art of Loving Yourself

Perhaps the most overlooked part of self-exploratory masturbation is the nurturing component. To a fault, we have this tendency to rush through most everything in our life. Self-stimulation is no different. Too often, masturbation is simply done as a quick, easy means to achieve orgasm. If we took our time and focused our thoughts and energy on the sensual pleasures our own touch can provide us, we would find self-exploratory masturbation to be extremely nurturing.

Susan's discovery of masturbation is typical of many of the female clients I've had over the years. She discovered masturbation quite by accident when she was a child. As she lay face down with a pillow between her legs she could move her body in such a way as to create an orgasm. This is the way Susan always masturbated, even as an adult. It was quick, efficient, and reliable. She usually did it at night before she fell asleep.

Susan came into therapy because she was having trouble lubricating during foreplay. Penetration was either very difficult or impossible without additional lubrication. She hated having to use lubrication and felt like a failure at sex. This problem was very disturbing to her social life, which she had greatly curtailed in order to avoid the embarrassment.

Susan described her feelings of "anesthesia" in the genital area when a man started touching her. She said she felt nothing. It didn't hurt, but it did not feel particularly good either. Mostly, genital touching by a man seemed more like a nuisance.

When I first asked Susan about masturbation, she said she never did it. Several sessions later she told me she hadn't been truthful because she was ashamed of the fact and the way in which she masturbated. She then told me about her pattern of using the pillow. We talked about her trying other methods, but she couldn't imagine actually touching her genitals with her hands.

What Susan needed was to be more sexually loving with herself so that she could allow another person to also love her. After many sessions exploring this concept, Susan agreed to try visualization in which she would imagine nurturing self-stimulation. Gradually Susan began to explore manual masturbation that was slow, explorative, and nurturing. She began alternating her pillow method with her own hand, adding an additional option to her sexuality.

As she took more time to nurture herself, she began to feel more open to dating again. On her first sexual venture she noticed that she wasn't nearly as uptight about being touched. For the first time, Susan let another person give her genital pleasure. She continued to date this man and her lubricating problem disappeared; so did her single life. She married him a year later.

Below is a visualization that will help you to love and nurture your sexual self.

▼

The Masterpiece

Imagine your body is a rare and extremely valuable sculpture. You are a collector of fine art and exploring in detail this masterpiece. You are thrilled to be able to put your hands on this truly marvelous composition. You can touch every part of it with gentle, loving care, glad to have the opportunity to be intimately involved with true genius. You explore its curves, slopes, and overall form, amazed at its natural beauty. You luxuriate in its various textures and know that this work of art is true inspiration. The genital area is design in its most creative form. You explore this part of the sculpture with intense amazement at the true genius of nature. You feel truly privileged to have this hands-on experience with such a one-of-a-kind masterpiece.

▲

Solo Sex and Partner Sex

You've already seen some examples of how masturbation is important to good sexual feelings about yourself and how this can add to partner sex. Something I haven't mentioned, however, is how masturbation in the *presence* of your partner can enrich your sex life.

In sex therapy, I often ask couples to consider trying mutual masturbation as a way to break down the barriers of embarrassment, shame, and guilt. As proof of the power of the taboos, most couples are extremely reluctant to even consider giving it a try. The few couples who do brave the taboos, report an experience far different from what they anticipated. Initially, they report a hesitancy, but once past the initial discomfort, they talk about how it helped them to feel totally accepted by the other person, how it brought them closer together, and how it made them feel safe. Instead of feeling foolish as they anticipated, they end up experiencing a closeness of a new kind.

Sharing the experience of breaking the ''rules'' is something that tends to bring us closer together. Remember back when you were a kid and you and a friend did something you weren't suppose to be doing. There was an element of anxiety about being caught, but you forged ahead. It could have been something as ''terrible'' as making a prank phone call or writing secret notes to a sweetheart. For days, you shared cryptic looks that intentionally excluded others, making your confidence even that more important. In those days, that was the ultimate experience of intimacy; being partners in ''crime'' acted like a knot, tying the two of you together. Breaking the taboo of mutual masturbation has the same effect; it bonds partners together.

The effects of this bonding are global; embarrassment, shame, and guilt around all of sexuality, not just masturbation, decreases. Our sexual thoughts, desires, and acts no longer feel like secrets we need to hide. We become more comfortable with our partners and feel freer to experiment in areas in which we formerly held back. This feeling of freedom adds an adventurous dimension to our sexuality, helping to counteract the feelings of un-involvement which inevitably lead to boredom.

Masturbating in front of a partner is not a prerequisite to a satisfying sex life. Many couples go their entire life together without it and never miss it. Like the magnificent sunset I spoke of before, it adds an intangible dimension to our lives; something above and beyond the ordinary. Also like the sunset, it's yours for the asking, free of charge. We simply have to be willing to go in search of it.

Below is a visualization that will help you to become more comfortable with being able to masturbate in front of your partner.

* * *

▼

The Invisible Wall

Imagine yourself naked, lying next to your lover. You're very turned on and ready for lovemaking. You reach out for your lover but find there is an invisible wall between the two of you. You can see your lover and your lover sees you, but you can't connect. You keep trying, but each attempt is met with repeated frustration. Finally you give up trying to reach your lover and instead begin to stimulate yourself. You're focusing only on yourself, blocking out everything around you. Your concentration is so intense that you feel free and uninhibited. All self-consciousness vanishes and your body responds with increasing pleasure to your own touch, finally culminating in an orgasm. As you slowly begin to become aware of your surroundings your lover comes back into focus. Instinctively, you reach out. The invisible wall is gone and your lover enfolds you in a warm, accepting embrace. You feel loved, cared for, and totally accepted.

▲

Masturbation with Intercourse

Combining masturbation with sexual intercourse is probably one of the best ways to achieve heightened arousal to the point of orgasm. However, like masturbation in front of a partner, many of us find we have a built-in resistance to this idea. We have a tendency to believe that this is a failure on our part to achieve orgasm the "normal" way. We also worry it may be insulting to our partner. The belief that our partner will feel like a failure if they don't give us an orgasm is very strong. No doubt, there are a few of us who do feel we are poor lovers if our partner uses masturbation along with intercourse. However, surveys indicate that only a small minority feels this way. Most of us find it to be a turn-on for our partner to stimulate themselves during intercourse.

Intercourse alone does not always provide the necessary stimulation to reach orgasm. Women, especially, find that additional clitoral or breast stimulation during intercourse gives them the arousal they need to reach orgasm. Men, too, often find that stimulation of the testes or their breasts during intercourse brings them to the level of arousal necessary for orgasm. Searching out your own particular pattern for the highest arousal is what will lead to satisfying sex. Masturbation during intercourse may help you to feel more fully aroused. It's worth a try.

Use this visualization to become more comfortable with using masturbation along with intercourse.

The Whisper

Imagine you and your lover are in the midst of intercourse. You're feeling very aroused but want to feel even more pleasure. You take your own hand and begin to stimulate yourself in a place and manner that you know will increase your pleasure to an even higher plane. Your lover whispers encouragement in your ear, telling you how arousing it is to see you giving yourself pleasure. This adds to your excitement and you continue to stimulate yourself and the pleasure mounts higher and higher until the tension is released in orgasm.

The Sexy Right-Brain World of Fantasy— Are You Ready for the Trip?

The premise of this book is that images produced by our imagination powerfully influence our behavior. Nowhere is this more effectively illustrated than in the use of sexual fantasy. You'll remember reading in chapter 1 that sexual fantasy is different from visualization. Sexual fantasy involves images that are erotic and intended to sexually arouse and create a change in your physiological response. Visualization, on the other hand, is directed toward a goal other than sexual arousal, even though the goal may be a sexual one: to relax as a lover, to be comfortable with masturbation, or to be less inhibited, for example.

Erotic fantasy has a dramatic ability to change our mood. We can be thinking about everyday tasks and then switch our thoughts to erotic images and easily become aroused within a matter of seconds. Simply reading an erotic scene from a magazine or book conjures up images that can suddenly turn us on. We can have the same effect from just closing our eyes and letting our imagination create an erotic picture. Fantasy's power to push out distracting thoughts has been documented by sex researchers. In fact, some of us can even orgasm through fantasy alone, although this is a behavior that comes from repeated practice.

It is extremely common to use sexual fantasy during masturbation. Fantasies are an excellent way for us to leave behind our unsexy, left-brain world. With practice, erotic fantasies can immediately take us away from routine activities and put us in exotic, exciting places. The combination of sexual fantasy and masturbation heightens our senses so that we are more able to concentrate and therefore more easily aroused. Because fantasy is concentration on eroticism, you'll find it easier to have an orgasm.

Sexual fantasies take a variety of forms, from romantic to very sexually explicit. You don't have to worry that your fantasies are harmful or wrong. Sexual fantasy will not cause you to act in discordance with your conscience. Just because you fantasize about sex with multiple lovers, for example, does not mean you would ever act on the fantasy. Nor does sexual fantasy about someone other than your partner mean you are being unfaithful.

Sexual fantasy is a delightful way to enhance your ability to become aroused. Erotic images will stimulate your right brain, helping you to relax and enjoy the pleasure. If you've never used sexual fantasy before, but want to, directed visualizations help you overcome whatever resistance might be in the way. Use this visualization to help you learn to use sexual fantasy.

* * *

Make-Believe

Imagine yourself reading a magazine or newspaper. You've just read the same paragraph twice and you realize you're not concentrating. You put down the magazine or newspaper and close your eyes. Erotic images come to your mind. As you play with those images for awhile, you begin to feel turned on. It's a good feeling to know pleasure can be so self-contained; you use your imagination to create pleasure. You feel comfortable knowing that images that are not real can still make you feel so good. You continue to experiment with the images and find that certain ones arouse you more than others. The arousal feels safe because it is under your mind's control and you've decided to let it flow.

Entrée into Our Right-Brain World

During masturbation we have the opportunity to leave behind the pressures of our everyday world and escape into a "time warp" of nurturing, sensuality, and pleasure. In one sense, masturbation is just another right-brain activity, like listening to music or truly enjoying the taste of a gourmet meal. If we take the time to savor the entire experience, we'll feel replenished. It's the difference between leisurely dining in a nice restaurant with lovely ambiance and great service and quickly stuffing a sandwich in our mouth while we're on the run. In both, we get fed, but in the former we get more than just nourishment; we also get nurtured.

Depleted, sometimes exhausted, from frequent giving of ourselves through working, parenting, partnering, and friendshiping, we need renewing. Right-brain activities fill up our empty cups. The wonderful thing about right-brain activity is that it allows us to get intimately involved. With music we get intimate with our sense of sound; with dining, our sense of taste; and with masturbation we can be intimate with all of our senses. Not much else in life offers us that exact opportunity with such convenience and at no cost.

It's not that an occasional quick orgasm isn't restorative. It certainly can be. It's best, however, to ensure that we have a variety of different alternatives. With nurturing sensual masturbation we continue to define who we are as a sexual person. With strictly pleasure-oriented masturbation we have easy orgasms. With partner sex, we safely share our self-exploration and our orgasms with another person. The combination of all three lends itself to the most long-term satisfying sex.

► CHAPTER 5

What Lust Does for Your Sex Life

▼

Passion, Urgency, Pleasure— The Fuel That Energizes Sexual Love

I like the poem below because it contains all the right-brain elements of lust: passion, laughter, urgency, pleasure, eroticism, and freedom.

> *I like the way you say my name*
> *I like the way your passion feeds my own*
> *I like the way you laugh*
> *The way your body touches mine*
> *Our blood moves with the same urgency*
> *The same hunger for pleasure*
> *Our minds dance through the night*
> *To the same erotic beat*
> *It's nice knowing you, now*
> *Now that we've grown into*
> *Our own free souls**

Only by delving into our right brain can we experience true lust. When we combine lust and an intimate

*Chereb, David M., *Night Dreams*. Lake Forest, Calif.: Merz Productions, 1986, 9.

connection with another human being, we get what I call sexual love—what great sex is really all about.

Lust is the fuel that energizes sexual drive. The best partner sex is full-force lusty sex. Lusty sex is sexual love that allows acceptance of human desires and pleasures. It's a love that respects and relates to the other person so there is no need for censors. Healthy lust does not harm so there is no need for restraint.

What makes lusty sex really great is the circular way in which it gives us permission to be uninhibited. The more our lust feels accepted, the more we feel free to give. As we give with abandonment, our partner feels freer to do the same. Under these circumstances, passion naturally builds in a spirallike fashion, escalating toward a surge of pleasure. This is nature's master plan for sexual love.

Unfortunately, the images of lusty sex often bring to mind the kind of sex you read about in the pulp books or see in the pornographic movies. This is not sexual love but rather self-absorbed, nonmutual, genitally focused sex. These models of sex are rarely examples of healthy lust because there is so little relatedness or sharing of pleasure. If these are some of the images you have when you think of lusty sex, this chapter will help you erase your slate and replace it with new images.

Sexual Satisfaction and Healthy Lust

Being comfortable with one's own lust is one of the key ingredients that makes the difference between long-term satisfying sex and sexual dissatisfaction. Studies of couples that have had an active, satisfying sex life over many years have shown one very important common element. All other things being equal, what these couples do that others don't is to value sexual pleasure. They are comfortable with their sexual desire, instincts, and passion—all of which make up the emotion known as lust. Because they attach no negative emotional baggage to their lust, they feel free to honor and celebrate their sexual needs. In doing so, sexual love becomes a priority and they make time in their lives to satisfy their lust.

The Mutual Exclusiveness of Guilt and Lust

Scientifically studying emotions is difficult because they are illusive and slippery. Because they emanate from the brain, where science is still in its infancy, it's difficult to document in detail how emotions operate. However, there is some early scientific evidence that does confirm the mutual exclusiveness of opposing emotions.

Most of our emotions originate in the hypothalamus, which is located in our brain stem. One main purpose of the hypothalamus is to act as a regulator so that our bodies maintain homeostasis. The hypothalamus coordinates the opposing actions of the parasympathetic and sympathetic nervous systems. We're most familiar with how this works as a thermal regulator of our body. If we're too cold, our heart rate is increased and our vessels constrict to return our body temperature back to normal.

The hypothalamus works in a seesaw-type fashion. It maintains an either/or system. For example, we cannot be too cold or too hot at the same time. Apparently, the hypothalamus regulates opposing emotions in the same way. We cannot love and hate at the exact same moment. Nor can we experience lust at the same time we experience guilt. Guilt, in a biological not moral sense, is an unhealthy emotion because it engages the sympathetic nervous system's response to fear. In doing so, it blocks the parasympathetic response of lust.

This blockage is experienced physiologically as a shutting down of the blood supply to the extremities. Because sexual arousal requires dilation of the vessels, arousal cannot coexist with any emotion that triggers fear. Guilt, shame, resentment, anger, and mistrust are all emotions that tend to engage the body's response to fear.

It's difficult for us to understand how this operates because we're simply not that aware of the physiology operating within us during emotional fear. For example, we don't experience fear, if we have to give a speech in the same way we experience fear if someone is holding a gun to our head. Guilt and shame reside more in our unconscious mind. Nonetheless, they exert a powerful influence over our homeostatic regulating mechanisms. To engage our lust, we have to purge our guilt.

Are You Part of a Sexually Lustful Couple?

Here's a list of behaviors that lustful couples do that unlustful couples rarely do. Honestly ask yourself which of these behaviors you consistently have in your life. If you score less than 50 percent, you'll have a better understanding why you might be dissatisfied with your sex life.

Sexually Lustful Couples:

- Intentionally stay in bed on a weekday or weekend morning and enjoy each other's company
- Watch less television in favor of a romp in the sack
- Let the laundry and lawn wait instead of their lust
- Are playful and uninhibited about their sexual desires
- Feel little rejection when one or the other is not in the mood because they know it won't be weeks or months before there is another opportunity
- Value sex too much to use it as a battleground for other areas of disagreement
- Recognize the need for transitions and so go out of their way to set a sexy, romantic mood with music, candles, oils, or special dinners
- Tease each other with innuendos to keep lust alive
- Are more experimental and willing to try new behaviors
- Are more likely to masturbate in front of their partner
- Enjoy sharing sexual fantasies and erotic talk
- Are more flexible in their conditions for sex, i.e., time of day, place, rules of cleanliness, etc.
- Communicate their sexual preferences to each other
- Are not ashamed to let their children know they have sexual needs
- Go into the bedroom, shut the door and tell the children they want private time

How Lust Develops—Take a Test and Discover Your Lust Quotient

How does one "get" lust? Are we born with it or does it "come" to us at some predetermined point in our life? Actually, adult lust *evolves* through a process, beginning at conception and ending only at death. We all have the potential to develop lust, but our life circumstances determine whether we fulfill that potential in adulthood. In order to understand the process, take a moment to do the following visualization.

The Flowering of Lust

Imagine your lust as a delicate seed that's been planted in the healthy soil of your brain. The seed is growing tiny roots. Now it is beginning to germinate and some very tiny, delicate leaves are emerging. Your new growth is receiving loving care. It's being watered, talked to, and given just the right amount of sunshine. It's beginning to grow bigger, the roots are really taking hold and new leaves are appearing. Soon your seedling is fully grown with many leaves and the beginning of a bud. Watch the bud as it slowly starts to open. It's beautiful in the way it unfolds and takes shape. It has many lovely colors, textures, and a delightful smell. Now it is a glorious flower that gives pleasure by its very being.

The "seed" of lust is planted in all of us at the moment of conception. Whether it develops into a mature, healthy flower depends on how it's nurtured in its youth. Just like a flower, the growth of lust is a daily process. The messages we receive from our interactions with ourselves and others act as nutrients to our flower of lust or as a defoliant that kills it.

Stages in the Development of Lust

The seed of lust begins *in utero* where genetic programming causes male or female hormones to be released at certain times throughout gestation. The exact contribution of fetal hormones to adult lust is unknown at the present. However, it is clear that the hormones do affect later sexual desires and functioning. Research in this area is ongoing and more specific information is bound to be available before the end of this century.

Up to age three, the development of lust is primarily dependent on sensuality and intimacy. Human touch is the infant and toddler's teacher—it serves as the first nutrient that helps the seed to develop roots. Touch that is comforting, reassuring, and nurturing communicates to the child that being close to another human being is not only safe but desirable. On the other hand, touch that is hesitant, ambivalent, anxious, or hostile introduces the feeling of being unsafe. This information about the nature of touch is stored away to be retrieved later when introduced to partner sex.

Somewhere around age three, the toddler starts becoming acquainted with the wonderful sensations produced by exploring the genitals. Self-exploration and curiosity "water" the seed and keep the roots alive. Questions about parents' genitals frequently arise, especially about the opposite-sex parent. It's also at this age that sexual rehearsal play with peers begins. "I'll show you mine if you'll show me yours" is a familiar phrase. Curiosity is the main motivator of these experiments. During this phase, a child develops a sense of positive or negative feelings about genital sensations. This phase normally lasts until age six or seven, when self-consciousness and awareness of social taboos act as inhibitors.

The next five years appear to be relatively quiet as far as sexual development. These are the years that Sigmund Freud called the latent years. Recently, however, sexologists have discovered that these years are anything but latent. It's during these years that much cognitive awareness is covertly being absorbed. Conclusions and assumptions about sexuality are formulated during this time as the child takes in and assimilates the varied messages that culture gives. Because most of the sexual learning is going on inside the child's mind, it only seems as if the child is totally uninterested in sexual matters.

This not-so-latent stage of sexual development is very crucial to future adult functioning. If the messages being absorbed are positive, the future outlook for healthy sexuality is good. Once adolescence explodes on the scene, sexuality becomes visible again. Hormones have a great deal to do with this and often simply overpower any social taboos. Obvious interest in appearance and opposite-sex peers predominate. It's a confusing time for teens. Secondary sex characteristics that accompany puberty cause extreme self-consciousness. Hormones are churning furiously, creating all sorts of new and exciting feelings. Interest in the opposite sex becomes a preoccupation.

The adolescent years are a time for teens to get their feet wet; ideally, a little at a time. It's a crucial time in the "rooting" of the flower of lust. Small doses of exposure to sexuality through masturbation, kissing, and petting prior to intercourse, allow the teen to slowly accommodate the powerful feelings that are generated by sexual arousal.

Without the hormones of the teen and young adult years, adult lust settles down into a more stable frame of mind. This does not mean that it need be stagnant. Adult lust stays alive and healthy only by continued nurturing. To keep your flower garden alive, you continually need to dig out the weeds. As indicated by the couples who have long-term satisfying sex, adult lust needs attention. It needs to be pampered, talked to, and treated with special care. Like anything in life, if you take care of your lust, it will stay in good shape and give you much joy.

The Development of Your Lust

Think back on your own experience and ask yourself the questions listed below. After you've asked yourself the question, let an image come to mind. Check the box in the *P* column in front of the question if a positive image comes to mind or the *N* box if the image is negative. Check the box under *DR* in front of the experience if you don't remember.

Touch, Ages Birth to Three

P N DR

☐ ☐ ☐ What were the messages I got from my family about touching?

☐ ☐ ☐ How much touching was there?

☐ ☐ ☐ Was it nurturing and affectionate?

☐ ☐ ☐ Was there any early sexual touching with a sibling, relative, or adult?

☐ ☐ ☐ How comfortable am I now with intimate touching?

☐ ☐ ☐ Is my comfort limited to certain situations? Certain people?

Masturbation, Ages Three to Six

P N DR

☐ ☐ ☐ What messages did I get about self-stimulation from family or religion?

☐ ☐ ☐ Was I ever discovered masturbating?

☐ ☐ ☐ What are my current feelings about self-stimulation?

☐ ☐ ☐ Do I feel entitled to enjoy self-stimulation with myself or with a partner?

☐ ☐ ☐ Was I ever exposed to adult masturbation and what impact did that have on me?

Sexual Rehearsal Play, Ages Three to Six

P N DR

☐ ☐ ☐ What was the attitude toward nudity in my home?

☐ ☐ ☐ What sort of sexual exploration did I do with peers?

☐ ☐ ☐ What did I learn about myself during this exploration?

☐ ☐ ☐ Did this prepare me in any way for adult partner sex?

☐ ☐ ☐ Was I ever discovered during sex play with peers?

☐ ☐ ☐ Were there any specific religious messages that influenced my thinking?

Cognitive Awareness, Ages Seven to Twelve

P N DR

☐ ☐ ☐ What discussions about sex did I have with my family?

☐ ☐ ☐ What discussions about sex did I get from my religion?

☐ ☐ ☐ What discussions about sex did I have with my peers?

☐ ☐ ☐ Did I read any books or magazines or see any movies or television that influenced my thinking about sex?

☐ ☐ ☐ Did I see any sexual contact between my parents or any adults that influenced my attitude toward sex?

☐ ☐ ☐ Were there any sex-education courses in school that affected my notions?

☐ ☐ ☐ Were there any particular sexual experiences with adults?

☐ ☐ ☐ Were there any particular sexual experiences with siblings?

Adolescence, Ages Thirteen to Twenty

P N DR

☐ ☐ ☐ How did I deal with the development of secondary sex characteristics such as voice change, breast development, pubic hair, changes in genitals, etc. ?

☐ ☐ ☐ How was the topic of sex dealt with in my family?

☐ ☐ ☐ Was I prepared for menstruation? What was the experience like?

☐ ☐ ☐ Was I prepared for wet dreams? What was the experience like?

☐ ☐ ☐ Were there any experiences of petting? How did these affect me?

☐ ☐ ☐ How was I introduced to the powerful feeling of sexual arousal? How did I handle these feelings?

☐ ☐ ☐ What was my experience with masturbation during this time?

☐ ☐ ☐ Was I concerned about pregnancy?

☐ ☐ ☐ What was my first experience with sexual intercourse like? (At whatever age.)

☐ ☐ ☐ Did I have any particular sexual experiences that strongly influenced my feelings about sex?

☐ ☐ ☐ Was I ever coerced into a sexual experience against my will? (This includes any experience that implied sex, not just sexual intercourse.)

First, total up your positive and negative experiences. Take a look at the overall messages and feelings you received throughout your development. Are they weighted more on the positive or negative side? Are they about even?

Most of us have never thought to correlate our development of lust with our current sexual satisfaction. Usually there is a fairly strong relationship. The more negative our experiences, the more likely sex will not be satisfying to us as an adult. Lack of satisfaction may be expressed through a particular dysfunction such as orgasm problems or erection problems or more generally expressed through lack of desire or its opposite, sexual compulsivity and partner plurality.

Conversely, the more positive our experiences, the more likely we are to be able to enjoy and to give it an appropriate balance in our lives. This is because the more conflict-free we are about our lust, the more natural and normal it will seem to us. Normalcy allows us to put it in the proper perspective.

If your positive and negative experiences balance out, you probably feel neutral about sex. If this is your situation, you could be easily influenced by your partner or partners. If you're connected with a "positive" person, you are likely to be swayed in that direction, or visa versa.

If your total contains many don't remembers, you've probably had a reason to block many of these memories from your mind. Think about your current sexual satisfaction. If you're very unhappy, you might have some past experiences that are extremely painful. If you want to do something to change your dissatisfaction, consider seeking professional help to explore these memories. Painful memories are best revealed with supportive, trained professionals.

If you've determined from the above questionnaire that you've experienced some messages about lust that are inhibiting you, do the following visualization to clean your slate.

▼

The Ugly Weed and the Beautiful Flower

Once again imagine your seed of lust as it takes root in your brain. The roots are delicate and just beginning to emerge. Next to your lust seed is a seed of shame and a seed of guilt, also beginning to take root. As your lust begins to germinate so does the shame and guilt, only they seem to be stronger and more tenacious than your lust. You can now tell that the seeds of shame and guilt are growing into ugly weeds. The stalk and leaves of your flower of lust keep trying to emerge, but the weeds of shame and guilt block your sunlight and sap your strength. The weeds of shame and guilt are overpowering your flower of lust, choking out its nutrients and depriving it of life.

Suddenly, deep from within the roots of your flower of lust, you feel a surge of energy and power. This surge of power comes from a determination not to let the ugly weeds overtake the beautiful, pleasure-giving flower. This is one situation in which the usually more obstinate and ugly weed will not win out over the more delicate and beautiful flower. Because of your determination, the roots of your flower of lust multiply in number and strength and now begin to wrap themselves around the roots of the weeds of shame and guilt, suffocating their supply of nutrients. Slowly the weeds begin to wilt and die, leaving behind only your glorious and pure flower of lust.

▲

Lust Revitalized—Some Success Stories

Thankfully, it's never too late to recapture lust. Below are four stories, each about a different interference with the development of lust, yet each demonstrates how to recapture the ability to experience sexual love.

Cathy

Cathy's story illustrates how early negative input was reversed later in life. Cathy grew up in a home with parents who didn't like each other very much. There was very little affection between them and there were lots of arguments, especially about the lack of sex. Her mother seemed to be in a bad mood a great deal of the time and her father was absent as much as he could arrange. Consequently, Cathy was pretty much left to grow up on her own.

Cathy had lots of boyfriends during high school but always kept herself distant when it came to sex. After all, she was deathly afraid of being labeled a "prick tease," the contemporary version of Eve. She believed, like many of her girlfriends, that women were not supposed to "tempt" men with sex if they weren't going to deliver, and she wasn't interested in delivering. Unknowingly, this fear was deadening her lust.

Because sex wasn't that appealing to her, restraining

her passion was easy. Besides, touching her genitals seemed so awkward and embarrassing she couldn't imagine doing it to a man. At twenty-two Cathy married and had her first experience with sexual intercourse on her honeymoon. Just as she suspected, it wasn't that great. Not surprisingly, she had married a man who was also uncomfortable with sex—he had never forced the issue during the two years they dated prior to marriage. It was one of the reasons Cathy felt he was the right man for her.

However, as the marriage progressed, Cathy learned that two "wrongs" don't make a right. Neither one was able to help the other grow sexually. Their sex remained awkward and very infrequent. Foreplay was severely limited to a little genital touching before intercourse. He was never able to last very long during intercourse and she was never able to have an orgasm.

After ten years of marriage and many talk shows later, Cathy finally asked her husband to go to sex therapy with her. He unequivocally refused. She begged. His response, which he carelessly let "slip," was to have an affair with another woman. Then, when Cathy confronted him, he told her that his new girlfriend didn't complain about his lovemaking. Cathy took the opportunity to ask for a divorce.

A year or so after the divorce she started dating again. After several unsuccessful short-term relationships, she met a man who was a gentle, patient, and caring lover. He was able to have intercourse for "hours"—or so it seemed compared to her husband. Still, Cathy was not able to have an orgasm. When she asked this man to go to therapy with her, he gladly accepted.

In therapy, we worked on Cathy's "lust quotient." She agreed to try reading erotic and sexy stories. She had expected to find them rather vulgar, but instead found that she could get turned on by them. This was an entirely new feeling for her—being turned on by the images in these stories. Could she bring this feeling to a loving relationship? She certainly thought it was worth a try. She began visualizing herself as the characters in the book, only she added the human-relatedness component to her images. At first there was a resistance to the mix, but with time Cathy began to feel "right" about blending lust with love. Cathy was discovering a whole new part of herself and she liked it. It was fun to share this previously hidden part of herself with a man who was so accepting. The barriers began to come down and the orgasms started to happen.

Connie

Connie's situation is another example of how visualization can "undo" years of the neglectful or negative images of lust. Connie is fifty years old. She's been married twice and divorced twice and she is now engaged to a man she adores. In her first two marriages, sex was mostly "unexciting—something I never really cared about." In her current relationship, sex is "pretty good, once I get into it. Usually, however, I'm not in the mood." Connie is in therapy because she feels her lack of interest in sex was the main reason her previous two marriages failed. She doesn't want to have another relationship fail on account of it.

She remembers no particular negative experiences in her sexual development. However, she described her mother as very Victorian in her views about sex. Connie was not allowed to date in high school and was always expected to be home by ten o'clock on the weekends when she was out with her girlfriends. In Connie's mind, it seems impossible that these few incidents in her history could be responsible for her lack of sexual desire. What she fails to realize, however, is that her mother's discomfort with sex was communicated to her in a thousand different covert ways. Antisexual messages were communicated, for example, in how Connie's mother dressed (and how she dressed Connie), what movies or television she allowed Connie to watch, her attitude about men, how she dealt with sexual jokes, how she felt about nudity in the home, and which of Connie's friends she liked and which ones she discouraged—all of these behaviors indicated, however subtly, that lust was somehow inappropriate.

When I asked Connie to visualize a truly lusty woman who enjoyed sex, what came to mind was a whore. Images of women in pornographic magazines immediately came to mind. The emotion attached to these images was disgust. She was surprised by these images and the powerful feeling it generated. Connie had never before consciously made the association between lust and disgust. For the first time ever, Connie realized that if she allowed her lusty feelings to emerge, she would feel like a whore. Finally, her lack of interest in sex began to make some sense.

To be able to enjoy feelings of lust, Connie needed to break the negative association. In Connie's case, we did this with a transference visualization in which something very positive in her life was transposed over her negative images. Fortunately, there was an activity in Connie's life that gave her great joy—dancing. She loved to dance and often would dance at home alone whenever the music called to her. She described dancing as something that made her feel free, full of energy, and totally in touch with herself. She used dance as a way to confirm her self-esteem. It was an activity that she did totally for herself—not something she did to please or placate others.

If she could feel this way about her lust, she would take as much delight in sex as she did in dance. Connie practiced visualizing herself dancing and experienced in her mind the joy she felt. Then she practiced transferring this emotion to the visual image of herself being totally lusty as a sexual partner. With repeated practice, Connie began to see lust as an emotion that could possibly cause joy instead of disgust. Her feelings of "I couldn't care less about sex" became instead, "Sex, like dancing, is a way I can feel good about myself."

Louis

Women, of course, are not the only ones who have trouble peacefully blending lust and love. Frequently, low sexual desire in men is usually related in some way to a discomfort with lust. There is one patient I will *never* forget because his story so vividly illustrates how vulnerable lust is to distortion.

My patient at age thirty-nine had the most lucid memories of how he was required at age seven to go to confession. Being only seven, Louis was naturally confused about exactly what sins were. He did remember, however, that the nuns had told him that touching his private parts constituted a sin. Knowing he was expected to have a sin, he manufactured his sin by intentionally playing with himself. Now he could go to confession and be "proud" that he had a sin to confess. In confession, he was told to say his Hail Marys for his sin and to never again transgress in this manner.

As often happens with the unsophisticated mind of a child, this whole process became distorted. Any thoughts about sex became associated with sin. It wasn't until Louis started dating as a teenager that the distorted association began to manifest itself in his inability to sexually connect with a woman. In each case, the sexual relationship would start out great. However, after a short time he would begin to lose interest in the sex, eventually feeling a revulsion toward it. Then he would end the relationship.

After fifteen years and a series of very unsuccessful relationships, Louis came to see me. Because he made his living as a writer, I had him keep a diary of his thoughts and images. His images were fraught with violence and rage, stemming from his pent-up anger at being forced to find shame and guilt in a behavior he enjoyed. Two and a half years later, Louis was finally able, with the help of written and visual imaging, to purge enough of his guilt to move forward in his life. He's at the point now where he wants to try another relationship. This time he's left behind the negative sexual images, which were causing his guilt, and he feels freer to truly engage in a meaningful one-to-one relationship.

Alice

Alice's situation is representative of a moderate aversion to sex. Alice described her childhood as normal and her parents as very busy but loving. Sex, however, was never a topic of discussion. Although Alice never remembers any negative messages from her parents about sex, she instinctively knew that topics of sexuality were not open to discussion.

The development of her lust was negatively influenced as a result of abuse from a neighborhood baby sitter. The sitter, a male, was five years older than Alice. The incidents happened when Alice was eight to ten years of age. What Alice remembers is being severely teased by this child. He would feign playing ''tag'' with her and chase her around the house. Eventually he would catch her and hold her down. Then he would make threats that he was going to rip her clothes off. He never did, but he seemed to enjoy tormenting Alice. His physical size and strength was scary and so were some of the pleasant genital feelings she had when he played these games. Part of Alice knew she should tell her parents about the incidents, but a larger part of her felt ashamed and afraid to bring up the subject. She wasn't that sure she wouldn't be blamed for participating.

Eventually the neighborhood sitter began dating and was no longer available to stay with Alice. Slowly Alice's memory of these incidents began to recede, or so she thought. It wasn't until she was married five years and in sex therapy because of low sexual desire that Alice realized the connection.

Alice told me she never remembered being very interested in sex. Her current husband had been her only sex partner. They had dated two years before they married, but even then the sex was only occasional and very marginal. She said she "never felt safe and therefore couldn't let go." Alice thought that it would get better once they were married and she felt more secure—then she would feel safe. She pressured John into marriage, promising that she would be a better sex partner once their relationship was legal. It never happened. John claimed that Alice "couldn't care less about sex. It might as well be the laundry she was doing."

Alice felt very guilty about disappointing John. Daily, she vowed to be a better wife. Yet, each time sex seemed eminent she would find an excuse or creatively avoid going to bed at the same time. Marriage did not wipe out the unsafe feeling as Alice had hoped. By the time they came into therapy, John had lost most of his patience. They fought a great deal about all sorts of things. Both of them knew, however, that they were really fighting about sex.

Through visualization Alice found both the cause and the cure for her aversion to sex. I asked Alice to visualize the most recent sexual experience she and John had. Once in the visualization, I told her to focus on the feeling of being unsafe. As she concentrated on this feeling, she was flooded with images of being held down and of being powerless. She felt a strong need to flee, but she was unable to escape. She began to recall memories of her male baby sitter and her current life began to make sense to her.

To reverse Alice's association between lust and powerlessness, Alice needed to break the association of feeling weak and out of control with being turned on. Alice was instructed to create an image of herself with the strength of Atlas. In her imagery she was no longer weak and unable to defend herself but rather totally in control. In the early visualizations, Alice was alone with her strength. Gradually John was added to her visualizations. She imaged herself feeling strong and in control while he was present. Then eroticism was slowly brought into her imagery until she could allow herself to feel sexually aroused and also feel strong enough that she was no longer a victim of a man's greater strength. Eventually Alice was able to feel safer with her sexuality—more in control. She no longer needed to deny her lust as a way to avoid feeling unsafe. The connection was broken.

It would be rare to get through the complicated developmental process of lust without one kind of detour or another. Yet, it's encouraging to know that the detours can be overcome by your own mental determination to do so. The distortions are created in your mind and therefore can be removed by your mind. Use this visualization to help you to mentally revitalize your lust.

The Garden of Eden

Imagine you and your lover are in the Garden of Eden. You are both naked. This garden is the most peaceful and comforting of places. In this garden you feel completely safe because your humanness is totally accepted. Completely surrounding you are luscious flowers giving off a delicious scent. These are the Flowers of Lust. As you drink in their aroma, you feel a sensuality beyond anything you have ever experienced. Your lover is also being aroused by the aroma of lust. Your lover's response excites you even further.

You look at each other's nakedness and enjoy the beauty of the human body. Your enjoyment increases your arousal even further and you feel a pleasant sensation in your genitals. You walk over and pick a Flower of Lust. As you do, the flower gives off a burst of its sweet perfume, which you deeply inhale. Every part of your body is tingling with erotic sensations. Your lover touches your body and you quiver with pleasure.

Never before have you felt such total abandonment. Reveling in the delight of your erotic response seems the most natural of human behaviors. In this garden, filled with the beauty of lust, you know this is the way nature truly designed men and women to feel. You experience your lust as natural, pure, and innocent. You're aware of a compelling desire to intimately and physically connect with your lover and to share the joy of giving and receiving lust. You both reach out to each other and are linked together in mutual, unconditional acceptance.

Spicy Soufflé of Lust—Served Hot

Imagine you are creating your own recipe for really great sex. Make out your shopping list. Write on the list:

To taste	Proper environment
50 cups	Fun
50 cups	Communication
Generous amount	Creativity
Unspecified amount	Time
Generous amount	Respect
Healthy dose	Concentration
All you can find	Lust

Now you are putting your ingredients together. Imagine yourself in a fifty-quart bedroom (or other suitable container) with the proper environment to your taste (distractions such as the phone or television will cause loss of flavor). Thoroughly stir together *fun* (really spicy sex is best when you play at it—not work at it—working at it causes an overdone, drab, and unappealing soufflé) and *communication* (your partner doesn't know what ingredients you like in your recipe). For best results throw in a generous amount of *creativity*. Add an unspecified amount of *time* and let simmer for as long as necessary. Quality cannot be rushed. For outstanding results, add a generous amount of *respect* (for yourself and your partner) and a healthy dose of *concentration* (enjoy the moment not the outcome). Cook over moderate heat until just before the boiling point.

Then turn up the heat by adding all the *lust* you can find. Continue to let it heat up but not boil. Then pour into your favorite soufflé dish and bake at 550 degrees until risen. Serve *hot*. Makes fifty quarts of sexual satisfaction—enough to last a lifetime.

► CHAPTER 6

Sexual Creativity Through Play

▼

Play—The Antidote for Sexual Boredom

Play is a right-brain activity. Without it, sex loses all its creativity. It's the spirit of play that allows us to feel the freedom of our imagination. When we play, we both imagine and create, expanding the dimensions of the self. When we play at sex, we engage our creativity and expand the dimensions of the *sexual* self. When you add play to intimate touch and lust, you get really great sex, the kind you never lose interest in.

Stop for a moment and let your mind drift toward an image of children at play. Pretend you're watching them through a telescope. Now zoom in closely and watch just one child playing. Notice the spontaneity of the child's activity and the total lack of self-consciousness. While there is interaction with other children, each child is really in a make-believe world of its own. Now zoom back and watch the total action going on. Hear the sounds. What you see and hear is an expression of the free spirit in child's play. *True* play is an expression of the self. *True* play helps us to maintain a perspective on other aspects of life and allows us to experience a balance between the joy and the difficulties life has to offer.

Sexual boredom is the number one complaint among couples who have been together for any length of time because adults don't play. When a child comes to a parent and says "I'm bored," what is the likely adult response? "Go play." Adults know that play is the antidote for boredom. The problem is that we think *true* play should only be the prerogative of children.

Letting Your Child Out to Play

Most of us have a misperception about adult play. When I speak of play, I'm not talking about playing a game of competitive tennis or cards. Adult games usually have rules, winners and losers, and, therefore, are not true play. True play is free of competition. I'm also not talking about spending leisure time reading, watching television, or going to the movies. These are activities without expression of spontaneity and although they may be relaxing, they are not play.

The following elements of play will help you differentiate true play from other apparent play activities:

- A spontaneity that results in loss of self-consciousness and is therefore free of judgment of the self and others
- A free-choice activity without obligations or constraints—you're playing simply because you want to
- A noncompetitive activity in which everyone wins and no one loses
- An active physical state in which the body is stimulated; the blood pressure and heart rate are accelerated during play and you feel exhilarated and refreshed—writing a creative poem may produce this state as well as a more physical action
- Play is unique to the individual so each of us may ascribe play to very different activities

- Play is a preoccupied state that engages and immerses us; we lose ourselves to the pleasure of the experience
- Humor and laughter rather than seriousness are hallmarks of effective play
- Relaxation is different than play because it reduces both physical and mental activity to a minimum; although this is healthy, it is not necessarily as spontaneous or joyous as creativity in play
- Feeling safe is a prerequisite to being able to play; if we feel threatened by physical harm or by being overpowered, our protective mechanisms are automatically engaged, and spontaneity and loss of self-consciousness become impossible

Take a moment to do the following visualization to help you get an image of adult play.

▼

A Game of Tag

You're on a beautiful beach. It's a warm, sunny day and the sky is a deep blue with many white puffy clouds. You're walking along the beach next to the water's edge and suddenly a wave comes up to your feet and almost catches you. As the wave recedes, you run after it as if in a game of tag. Then another wave starts to roll in and you run just far enough away from it to avoid being caught. Then you start to chase the wave as it rolls once again out to sea. There are hundreds of people on the beach but you are totally unaware of anything other than yourself and the waves. You feel a lightness of spirit and the world seems joyous. You're laughing at the waves and you are engaged in a world of your own. You can feel your heart racing and a slight excitement in your body as you and the waves interact in total nonjudgmental non-competitive relatedness. No one is telling you how to play with the waves or for how long. No one is giving you a grade and there is no winner or loser. There is just you, the waves, your spontaneity, excitement, laughter, and joy.

▲

How to Make Friends with Play and Lust

Play and lust are very close friends. They walk hand in hand and, as good friends do, support each other in building a stronger sexual self. Both play and lust are instinctual parts of us and can be observed in all cultures throughout history. This is an indication of their univer-sality. *If lust is the core emotion that drives our sexuality, then play is the vehicle that gets us where we're going.* Without play, lust is left standing alone with nowhere to go.

The following visualization will help you better in-tegrate both lust and play into your sexual self.

* * *

▼

Merging Clones

Imagine you are slowly walking alongside a clone of your-self. You're both headed toward your lovers and anticipate a sexual encounter. You're about two feet apart and can see each other but can't touch. The two of you are identical except for the shirts you are wearing. One of you is wear-ing a shirt that says lust *and the other a shirt that says* play. *Although you are both walking in sync, you don't feel as one. You're looking forward to the sexual encounter so you both try to pick up the pace, but you feel lethargic, unable to motivate yourselves.*

You look at each other and know that as one you would feel more energized. Yet, the small distance between you seems like a vast empty space. To close the space you take a step toward each other. Now you reach out and take hold of each other's hands. When you touch, you feel a surge of energy pass between the two of you. You feel stronger, more enthusiastic and are now able to move more rapidly toward the sexual rendezvous with a united lover.

▲

Balancing Play Against Obligation

Now that you have both a visual and written notion of what play is, think about how playful a person you are. Evaluate how much play you have in your life by asking yourself the following questions. In the last year, when was the last time:

1. I acted totally spontaneously without fear of judgment?
EXAMPLE: Sang out loud because I felt like it.
2. I had a big belly laugh or laughed until I cried?
3. I was so preoccupied in something joyous that I blocked out the rest of the world.
EXAMPLE: I unplugged the phone during lovemaking.
4. I engaged in a noncompetitive activity with another person simply for pleasure and fun?
EXAMPLE: I played "footsie" under the table.
5. I totally abandoned self-awareness in favor of the moment?
EXAMPLE: I had a brainstorm and shared it without concern for its acceptance.
6. I let the child in me overshadow the adult in me?
EXAMPLE: I took an extra five minutes from my obligations to daydream or play make-believe.

If you're having trouble remembering a specific time, you're not alone because few of us appropriately balance play against obligation. We spend too much time in our left brain dealing with the many demands life deals us. At some level, most of us know we don't have enough play in our lives. However, it's so very easy to feel that our obligations *should* take priority over play. Shoulds make us feel guilty when we take time out for play, usually labeling it frivolous and something only children are allowed to do.

Here's a visualization that will help you better balance play against obligation.

* * *

The Seesaw

Imagine there are two of yourself, each sitting on opposite ends of a seesaw. One of you represents the part of you that responds to demands and obligations and the other one of you represents your playful self. The two parts of you are unbalanced; the playful part is way up in the air and the obligation part, down on the ground. The part of you that is up in the air feels out of touch with the real world down on the ground. It feels without substance and you realize you haven't given it enough weight to counteract the heaviness of the obligations you feel.

Now imagine the obligations you feel as rocks in your pocket. Take out a few rocks and drop them on the ground. As you do this, the seesaw starts to move and the obligation part of yourself starts to feel lighter and begins to lift off the ground. Keep taking out the obligation rocks a little at a time until you see the two parts of yourself have perfectly balanced themselves. Now the obligation part of yourself feels lighter and the play part of yourself feels of more substance and able to balance the obligation part. The two parts of you now feel centered with both parts having their feet on the ground.

Inviting Your New Friends
to Play in Your Backyard

Have you every noticed how much easier it is to be playful on a vacation away from home? It makes sense. Vacations are the only time we're given "permission" to play. With most of us having only two weeks for vacation, it's no wonder we are not a playful bunch. When we do manage to play in our own backyard instead of having to go away on vacation, we feel guilty, as if we're cheating.

There are two main reasons we feel guilty about playing. The first is that all of us were raised in a culture that endorses a very strong work ethic. Much of our self-esteem revolves around how productive we are. Accomplishments are rewarded with status, money, and even engraved plaques. I know of no trophies that are given for being able to play.

The second reason we have trouble playing has to do with our world view—our basic perspective on life. World views exist on a continuum from positive to negative. Most people tend to be at the same point on the continuum in most aspects of their life. We all know people who are negative about just everything or are Pollyannas about everything. The majority of us falls somewhere in the middle. A few of us bounce around on the continuum, depending on a particular aspect of life. Unfortunately, most of us tend toward a negative world view when it comes to adult play. Play is for children, not adults. The negativity is expressed in attitudes of feeling silly, childish, trivial, or flighty about playing.

Turn back a few pages and read once again the list of elements that make up play. Sex is one activity that presents the opportunity to have all of these elements. Unfortunately, our negative attitude about play restricts us from feeling playful about sex—as well as many other aspects of our lives.

Ralph and Sara's attitudes about play are typical of many of the couples who have little sex in their lives. They've been married eight years. Ralph is forty-eight and Sara is forty-four. Ralph was married before and brought two teenagers to their new household. Sara looked forward to raising the two boys. As you might guess, however, it was not smooth sailing. Adolescence is a time of separation and individuation and, not surprisingly, the boys did not easily take to a new authority figure in their life. Unconsciously, Ralph felt protective of the boys and came across as nonsupportive of Sara's attempts at being a mother.

It wasn't long before dissension in the household was a constant theme. The glorious sex that had characterized Ralph and Sara's early relationship soon vanished. It was replaced by no sex at all. Wise enough to know they needed some help, they sought family therapy. It took two years of hard work, but they learned how to compromise on issues of stepparenting and the tension in the household greatly diminished.

They came to sex therapy two and a half years after they finished family counseling. The boys were both grown and out of the house and Ralph and Sara were getting along better than ever. So, it puzzled them why they were still not having sex. When I saw them, it had been eight months since their last sexual encounter. Before that it had been six months. Ralph's comment was "at the rate we're going, we'll get in the Guiness Book of World Records in about ten years."

On the surface, it was a mystery why they had so little sex. They were getting along well and had no major resentments toward each other. Ralph was doing very well in his career and told me, "For the first time we have money for little extras. These should be the Golden Years.'' I asked Ralph to tell me more about his work.

As it turned out, he had received a promotion three years earlier. It was what he always wanted and was thrilled to finally be where he aspired to be—at the top of a large corporation where he had no boss to tell him what to do.

I asked him what he did for relaxation and play.

He gave me a blank stare. ''Relaxation? Play? As it is, I'm only getting about five hours of sleep a night,'' he told me.

''So if you felt sexy, when would you fit it in?'' I inquired.

''On a weekend, I guess,'' he said hesitantly.

''You don't work on the weekends?''

''Well, actually I do. I have a lot of paperwork that I catch up on over the weekend. And, of course, there is lots to do around the house.''

''This may seem like a switch in gears,'' I said, ''but I'd like to know what you remember about your childhood years of play. Close your eyes for a minute and go back in time to when you were ten years old. What do you see yourself doing on Saturdays?''

''What comes to mind is my father waking us kids up early with a knock on the door and yelling, 'Up and at 'em.' You know—like a sergeant in the Marines.''

''Was your father a Marine?''

''No, but he sure acted like one at times. He was quite a taskmaster. The weekends were for getting things done and he had a list of chores that kept us very busy.''

''Kind of like now, huh?'' I asked.

At this point, I noticed Sara was really getting restless. I asked her what was on her mind.

''What the two of you are talking about is making me uncomfortable because I'm beginning to see a little of myself in all this. I've got every minute of Saturday and Sunday planned out for accomplishing what I didn't get done during the week. And I'm beginning to see your point. It's a little scary. We're both into a way of life that doesn't allow for anything that isn't productive—including sex. Is there something we can do?''

''Well, I'd like you to consider trying an experiment. This weekend I want you to both stay in bed on Saturday or Sunday morning for an extra hour. Don't even think about sex. Just see if you can stay in bed and talk, read the paper or something relaxing. That does not mean doing paperwork from the office.''

The next week, Ralph and Sara canceled their appointment. Ralph was away on business. As Sara explained on the phone, Ralph's traveling was a common occurrence and an important part of his responsibilities. In the following session we talked about Ralph's traveling. It wasn't the first time they both acknowledged that his being away was part of the problem, but it was the first time they saw it as an overall pattern in their lives. Work almost always took precedence over play. It was a basic philosophy of their lives and they began to see how the decisions and choices they made were based on this philosophy. They were reassigned the previous ''homework.''

On their own, they decided to go away for the weekend to try the assignment. Getting away would help, they thought. It did. When they returned for the following session they were both smiling. Instead of their usual vacation that consisted of ''up and at 'em'' and cram everything you can into one day, they stayed in bed on Saturday morning and for the first time in over eight months had sex. Both Ralph and Sara expressed delight—and frustration. They were thrilled that they had broken the awkwardness of sexual abstinence, but they were concerned that they had to leave home to do it. Would they always have to go away in order to have sex? Why couldn't they play in their own backyard? To answer that question, we took a look at their "anchors" to play and to sex.

Anchors That Help, Anchors That Hinder

Ralph and Sara's situation illustrates the power of "anchoring"—the human tendency to respond in the same way when surrounded by the same stimuli. In our homes, the work that needs to be done serves as an anchor or a reminder of what we haven't accomplished. So a pile of laundry, professional journals, or bills actually activate our left brain. It takes a concentrated effort to move into our right brain when surrounded by such anchors. Going away on vacation means leaving the anchors behind—out of sight, out of mind. That's why vacations make it so much easier to be in our right brain and why sex happens more often.

Of course, most of us can't take weekly vacations. We can, however, have right-brain anchors to counteract the left-brain ones. Certain anchors that make us think of sex are very familiar to us because they've been immortalized by books and movies. Romantic dinners, flowers, candlelight, music, and lingerie are some of the more well-known anchors (and usually much more available on vacation). With a playful spirit, our creativity can be released to develop our own unique countering anchors. This is what Ralph and Sara were asked to do.

They were to remove all reminders of work from the bedroom. None of Ralph's undone paperwork was to be in that room. Nor was Sara to have any reminders of her undone lists in the bedroom. Together, they went on a playful shopping trip during which they bought sexy outfits for their new "playpen." When one or the other felt sexy, they put the outfit on the bed to signify their mood. Sara started to buy funny cards for Ralph to have when he came home from a long day. Ralph took two five-minute breaks during each day to visualize a playful, sexy scene with Sara. Not surprisingly, some of the spontaneity, playfulness, and passion of their early sexual relationship returned.

Will Ralph and Sara's new sexual vigor last or is it simply artificially created by being in therapy? The answer depends, of course, on how motivated they are to change. Changing the anchors will help, but the long-term success comes from a willingness to value play. If we believe in the value of play and use the strategies of change outlined in chapter 2, we will naturally balance play against obligation (and productivity).

Is It Really Possible to Keep Sexual Passion Alive?

Ask yourself, When was the last sexual experience you had in which you let go of control long enough to feel like a free spirit with total lack of self-consciousness? Do you remember teasing, laughing, and, perhaps, even giggles? For most of us, playful sex naturally occurs early in new relationships—we never even have to think about it. Also, for most of us, the play component of sex slowly fades away over time.

There has been much written about the way in which relationships change over time. With regard to sex, the disappearance of spontaneity, play, and passion is legendary. Also quite familiar to most of us is the feeling of boredom that often replaces the loss.

The question that most of us want answered is, Are

the changes inevitable? The answer is yes *and* no. Yes, there are certain unavoidable changes that occur as a relationship matures. And, no, boredom is not a mandate of these changes. We do have other choices. Let me explain.

In a relationship's infancy and youth, spontaneity and play are as natural as the above-imagined scene of the children playing. As a relationship develops and grows, it replicates life. That is, with maturity comes responsibility and dealing with real-life demands such as differences in values, habits, preferences, backgrounds, religions, and the myriad of other issues that become the focus of mature relationships.

As children, we watched adults deal with any demands, irritants, or roadblocks by directing negative energy toward them. The western way of dealing with life's demands has always been to see them as the enemy—something that needs to be fought, conquered, and controlled. Struggling is revered. Thus, we see daily life as a battle.

Unfortunately, we also tend to treat relationship demands in the same way. In the inevitable evolutionary development of relationships, demands become something we unknowingly treat as the enemy. Dealing with the enemy is stressful.

This is how we introduce stress into our lives. Too much stress can inhibit sexual desire—the one activity that can nurture us and actually reduce stress. Most of us feel this void and in an effort to get sex back in our lives, we often add it to our list of obligations to be achieved. We search for a time somewhere between our jobs, our children, our relatives, our friends, our organizations, and our recreation. It's a circular strategy that escalates rather than reduces stress because sex starts to feel like just one more left-brain chore.

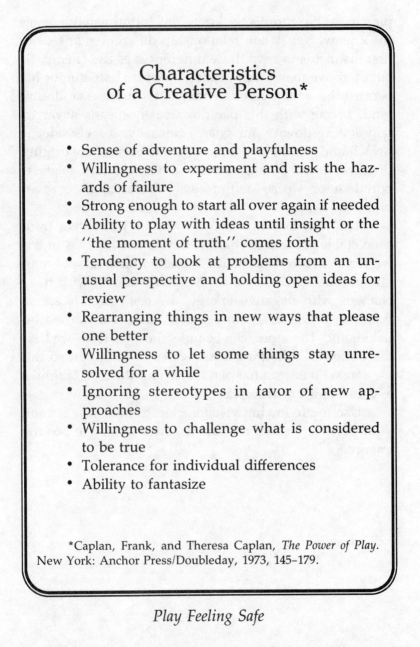

Characteristics of a Creative Person*

- Sense of adventure and playfulness
- Willingness to experiment and risk the hazards of failure
- Strong enough to start all over again if needed
- Ability to play with ideas until insight or the "the moment of truth" comes forth
- Tendency to look at problems from an unusual perspective and holding open ideas for review
- Rearranging things in new ways that please one better
- Willingness to let some things stay unresolved for a while
- Ignoring stereotypes in favor of new approaches
- Willingness to challenge what is considered to be true
- Tolerance for individual differences
- Ability to fantasize

*Caplan, Frank, and Theresa Caplan, *The Power of Play*. New York: Anchor Press/Doubleday, 1973, 145–179.

Play Feeling Safe

By definition, the enemy is someone that can't be trusted and certainly not someone we feel safe to invite to be our playmate. We intuitively know not to intimately engage the enemy. Yet, when relationship differences arise, our first instinct is to treat these differences as the enemy. So although we may love our mate, we also hate him or her because he or she is our enemy. It's the classic double bind. Living with this paradox usually means never totally letting down your guard. Sexually, it feels safer to detach and withhold. So we've come back to the original premise: Lack of engagement almost always leads to boredom or worse—withdrawal, dysfunction, or even vindictiveness.

Yes, relationships will always go through a fairly predictable process of change. In relationships, as in life, we never get to keep youth's totally unjaded, spontaneous infatuation. But we do not have to deal with these changes with negative energy. *We don't have to see demands or differences as our enemies.* These are learned behavior and, therefore, can be unlearned. Instead, we have the option of reframing what we've been taught so that we can keep our sexual playmates and the fun, laughter, and free spirit of true play.

Use the following visualization to help you reframe your perspective and convert negative energy to positive energy.

* * *

Foe to Friend

You and your lover are in one of your favorite environments for a sexual encounter. The ambiance is just right. You're feeling relaxed, safe, and in the mood for a great sexual experience. Suddenly, your lover says or does something that irritates you. Somehow a very sensitive "button" has been pushed and you're aware that your mood has changed. Your concentration has drifted away from feeling sexy; your arousal has vanished. Instead, you're getting angry. You feel injured and the feeling of safety has disappeared. It's replaced by an instinctual part of you that wants to hurt back. Your lover has been transformed into your enemy with horns, a pitchfork, and an evil countenance.

You suspend all action for three seconds. You don't say or do anything. Then you look closely at your lover. Behind the horns and the evil countenance you see a vulnerable person. You realize the remarks or behavior were not meant to irritate or hurt you and there was no evil intent. The horns, pitchfork, and evil countenance disappear and are replaced by a pleasant smile. This person looks friendly and loving. Now you remember why you were together in the first place. Your concentration returns and you are once again able to focus on the eroticism, pleasure, and joy of the encounter. You move your body close to your lover's and prepare for a flood of warmth to envelop your body as the two of you touch.

Verbal Aphrodisiacs

The language of sexual love is an important part of sex play. Language creates a mood and therefore is an important part of giving a message that playing is acceptable. Children are straightforward about the message. "Do you want to play?" they ask. Adults rarely ask another adult, "Do you want to play?" They may ask a sexual partner, "Do you want to fool around?" That's about as close as any adult gets to asking another adult to play. For most of us, playing is rarely associated with sex and, therefore, our language doesn't reflect playful images.

It's interesting to note that the search for an external aphrodisiac such as a pill or drug has preoccupied us for centuries. We've not yet been successful in our search. Yet, all the time the most powerful aphrodisiac resides at home, in our right brain, waiting like Sleeping Beauty to be aroused by the right words and images. Language is one of the most powerful aphrodisiacs because words are immediately translated into images that act as sexual stimulants.

Learning to use the words to create the images can dramatically change sexual behavior. For years I have tried to get couples to engage in playful, erotic talk as a way to both get turned on and to communicate their sexual preferences. The resistance has always been strong. Erotic talk for most people brings to mind an image of "dirty." Naturally, this image makes many people uncomfortable. The solution for this dilemma is to settle for nonverbal communication. Unfortunately, it's a solution fraught with problems.

Nonverbal communication is at best risky. What does a moan mean for example? How do we gauge a nonverbal message such as a stroke, kiss, or caress? Is a kiss just an expression of affection or is it a prelude to something more erotic? Countless affectionate but non-sexual opportunities are ruined by a misperception that eroticism was the hidden agenda. An equal number of marvelous sexual situations are sabotaged in the same way. Here's a situation described to me by one of my patients.

It was early morning and Scott and Maureen were still in bed. Maureen was feeling playful and sexy. Scott's back was to her so she reached out to stroke his back. Scott stirred, gave a moan, but didn't turn over or touch Maureen. Now Maureen was uncertain whether to proceed. "Maybe he just isn't in the mood," she wondered. "Last time I reached out in the morning to try to get something going, he started touching my breasts, but then fell back asleep." She was hurt by his rejection. The hurt immediately turned into anger that lasted for days and ended in a big fight. She didn't want to be hurt again so rather than risk a rejection, she thought she would just forget it.

Later that night, Scott started to pick a fight with Maureen. It seemed to come out of nowhere. "What's going on?" she asked. Finally, he said that he was upset because she started something that morning but didn't finish. He didn't know if her stroke meant she was in a sexual mood or just being affectionate. He also remembered how angry she was when he fell asleep and he didn't want to upset her if she wasn't giving him a sexual message. A perfectly playful mood and opportunity for sex was ruined by vague nonverbal communication. Unfortunately, it happens millions of times each day in bedrooms around the world.

This situation could easily have been averted if Maureen had said to Scott (while stroking his back), "I'm feeling turned on this morning, could I interest you in some great sex?'' Because Scott was in the mood, the invitation would have been gladly accepted. But what if Scott wasn't in the mood? Then Maureen would have to deal with the big ''R'': *rejection.*

Bedroom Lingo*

For a uniquely playful experience in sexual communication and intimacy, play the following game with your lover. On a sheet of paper, guess what your lover might answer to the following questions. Then share and discuss your answers. Be prepared to get turned on.

1. Favorite time for sex:
   What time does your body clock say, when it most wants a roll in the hay?
2. A place for sex:
   Using your imagination, create the perfect location.
3. Sexual invitation:
   When you know he or she desires you, what kind of approach most inspires you?
4. Sexual initiative:
   When you know that you want to do it, who do you feel should lead the way to it?

*Special thanks to Orin Solloway for the imaginative and playful use of sexual language through rhyming.

5. Beginning foreplay:
When desire is about to burst, what is your favorite thing to do first?

6. Initial arousal:
Can you describe the special move, that gets you into a sexual grove?

7. Favorite foreplay:
While the process of foreplay delights you, which is the part that most excites you?

8. Masturbation:
Do you believe it can be grand, to lovingly take yourself in hand?

9. Sex talk:
When it comes to a sexual occasion, what do you think of erotic conversation?

10. Sexual fantasy:
Do you find any great ecstasy, in sexual fantasy?

11. Sexual concentration:
While engaged in a sexual escapade, what sort of things might cause your ardor to fade?

12. Sexual positions:
Belly to belly or front to back, your favorite pose for a romp in the sack?

13. Favorite strokes:
What particular tickle or touch, in which particular fashion, is most likely to stir your particular passion?

14. Sexual techniques:
Would you like your lover to pay more attention to certain details you haven't mentioned?

Play Overcomes Rejection

Fear of the big "R" kills eroticism and fear of rejection is one of our most basic fears. Like guilt, fear cannot coexist with lust. It's another either/or situation. However, very few of us have enough self-esteem to be totally fearless when it comes to rejection—especially sexual rejection. Like Maureen, we would rather forego sex than take the risk.

As a strategy to avoid rejection, we use nonverbal communication. We fool ourselves into thinking that nonverbal messages mean we will experience less rejection. A nonverbal message is only implied. The thinking is that if we don't *say* it, we don't have to take responsibility for it. Maureen's unconscious plan was that if she just reached out to Scott rather than said anything, he might pick up her desires through ESP or some other magic communication. She wasn't really owning up to being the one who wanted sex and perhaps she could get Scott to be the one to turn over and start something. That way she wouldn't feel rejected because she never clearly stated her intention.

As you can see, Maureen's plan backfired. A plan like this usually does. First, because it's so convoluted and dishonest and second, because the average person is not equipped with ESP and, therefore, can't clearly read a nonverbal message. Scott responds back in a nonverbal way and the potential for miscommunication is doubled. In trying to avoid taking responsibility for our own sexual desires, we rarely avoid rejection. Instead, we inadvertently avoid sex. It's a vicious cycle that escalates toward severe relationship problems.

Learning to be more playful with our sexuality is one very important way to deal with the feeling of rejection. Playful sexual language rather than nonverbal ambiguities is a much better solution. Getting rid of the image of sexual language as dirty and replacing it with playful images will help to improve sexual communications. Let's go back to Maureen and Scott and see how this might work.

Maureen has said to Scott, "I'm feeling turned on this morning. Could I interest you in some great sex?" She's clearly stated her sexual desire and invited, without setting an expectation or demand, that Scott join her. Suppose he either isn't in the mood or doesn't feel he has time? If he playfully reaches over to Maureen and says, "I love it when you turn into a sexpot, but this morning isn't good for me. How about we make a date tonight. That way I can think about you all day. By tonight I'll be crazy for you." Scott has both accepted Maureen's sexual desires and confirmed his interest in her. Consequently, Maureen will probably experience disappointment but not rejection. Disappointment is much easier to handle.

Is this romantic fantasy or romantic reality? It's a reality for those couples who (1) honor and accept their lust, (2) let play engage their creativity and guide their communication, and (3) use positive sexual imagery to keep their desires alive. That's what right-brain sex is all about.

Use the following visualization to help you both engage your playful sexual self and to image sexual language as playful.

* * *

The Giant Playpen

Imagine your favorite sexual place as your own giant play-pen. Put any sexual toys you want in the playpen. Now imagine you and your lover as playmates in the playpen. Ask your lover to come over and play. While you're touching each other in a sensual way, you're also talking. You're teasingly taking turns telling each other what you're going to do to arouse the other to the point of not being able to stand it. There's lots of laughter as you each try to find something more arousing than what was previously said. As the fun mounts, so does the eroticism. You feel alive with relatedness and excitement.

Summary of Ways
to Engage Your Playful Sexual Self

1. Practice the visualizations in this chapter in order to

- Integrate lust with play
- Better balance play against productivity
- Learn to tolerate individual differences by turning enemies into friends
- Image sexual language as playful, not dirty

2. Be aware of your anchors that hinder and help and use them to enhance your sexual responsiveness

3. Remember about the need for transitions from left brain to right brain, allow time and appropriate activities; the more playful the activity, the better
4. Enjoy and play with your fantasies and dreams
5. Minimize fear of rejection by adopting a playful spirit

► CHAPTER 7

Pleasure:
The
Final
Destination

▼

If lust is the fuel that energizes sexual drive and play is the vehicle that takes us where we're going, then pleasure is the final destination. Pleasure gives meaning to life; without it we feel empty and without purpose. The anticipation of pleasure leads to internal motivation to achieve satisfaction through work, play, love, and sex. Like lust and play, we're all born with the potential to experience great pleasure. Unfortunately, as with lust and play, many of life's roadblocks prevent us from reaching our destination. Too many of us live with too little pleasure.

Pleasure is a sensation; to experience it we have to be in touch with our bodies. We know pleasure only by being connected with our five senses. For example, there is pleasure in the *smell* of good food cooking, the *sight* of someone we've missed, the *feel* of something soft against our bodies, the *sound* of great music, and the *touch* of a loved one.

Exercise: Your Personal Pleasure List

Make a list of the things that give you pleasure. Really give some thought to the simple, everyday experiences that make you feel good. Taking your shoes off at the end of the day, for example. Once you make your list, you'll notice that it is impossible to define pleasure without referring to the senses. Making this list will not only put you in touch with how much you tend to take these small pleasures for granted, but will also elevate your awareness of how much you depend on your senses for the experience of pleasure.

Are You in Tune with Your Body?

Because true pleasure is associated with the body, the experience of pleasure means letting go of conscious control so that the body responds freely. Pleasure is experienced only in the moment in which the sensation is occurring. We can anticipate the pleasure of the taste of chocolate, but we experience it only at the moment in which the chocolate is in contact with our sense of taste. Pleasure, therefore, is not subject to command or to the will. It's a ''happening'' of its own—as anyone who has made extensive preparation to have it can tell you: It won't be had. To have it, we must surrender to it because pleasure takes possession of us, not the other way around.

Like all pleasure, *sexual* pleasure is experienced only in the moment. If we let our mind drift away from the sensations that are generating our pleasure, the pleasure disappears. For example, if you're eating a piece of chocolate and somehow get distracted, you won't enjoy the taste sensation. The same is true with sexual pleasure. Distractions interfere with the sensations and inhibit physiological arousal. During sex, *thinking rather than feeling takes us out of the moment.* Even thinking about whether our partner is enjoying the experience, for example, will cause us to lose pleasurable sensations.

Can You Surrender to Pleasure?

Although each of us will have had somewhat different experiences with pleasure, there are three general categories of experiences with which we all must successfully deal in order to enjoy sexual pleasure. These are

* A belief in your ability to survive pain
* A surrender of power to pleasure
* Balancing your own pleasure against pleasing others

These three conditions are linked together in a circular fashion. Here's how they interrelate.

The Pleasure-Pain Continuum

If genetic programming goes smoothly, every human being is born with the capacity to experience sensations through their five senses. As mentioned, our senses allow us to experience pleasure. What makes the whole process so complex is that these same senses also allow us to experience pain. An infant's sensation of hunger, for example, is experienced as pain; the sensation of fullness is experienced as pleasure. Because of their close association, the anticipation of one may immediately give rise to the anticipation of the other.

With this example, it's not difficult to see how easily our need for food may get out of control. Hunger signals our bodies by producing an unpleasant sensation. To avoid the unpleasantness, we satisfy the hunger and experience pleasure instead. Soon, we come to *anticipate* that hunger will create an uncomfortable sensation. If we have a low tolerance for the pain of hunger, we unconsciously avoid the anticipation of this pain by eating when we're not hungry or eating more than needed as a way to stave off the anticipated pain. The more we avoid the pain of hunger, the less tolerance we have for it and the more we anticipate the need to avoid it. It's a circular process that builds on itself. Sometimes, in a contradictory fashion, we starve ourselves as an attempt to "have the pain before it has us."

We can do the exact same thing with sexuality. In infancy, nurturing touch provides us much pleasure, its absence much pain—experienced as loss, abandonment, frustration, or humiliation. Because few of us ever get through infancy and childhood without some experience of loss or abandonment, we all have some degree of fear that we'll have to experience this pain. These same painful emotions can be experienced at any point in our life whenever we experience loss, hurt, or rejection from someone we've totally given ourselves to. We instinctively try to avoid these painful emotions by not being connected to our feelings. In the process we diminish our capacity for feeling love, joy, and pleasure. The more we avoid experiencing these painful emotions, the lower our tolerance for pain. If we have experienced a traumatic loss or many losses we will have a tendency to avoid pain by not allowing ourselves to be connected to another person. We unconsciously sabotage any relationship that threatens to be intimate. We "leave" before they can leave us.

Or, we may do the opposite by continually searching for pleasure through frequent sex and/or multiple partners. The search becomes compulsive because, in reality, its motivation is to alleviate pain, not experience pleasure. Sex acts like a "fix" and, as with all addictions, we continually need more to ward off the anticipation of pain that inevitably comes when the fix has worn off. However, compulsive sex provides only momentarily suspension of pain, never pleasure. We may have lots of sex, but very little sexual satisfaction. So the search must continue.

In the absence of disease or trauma, our inability to experience sexual pleasure occurs because we are unable to let go of conscious control of our bodies. We unknowingly block our pleasurable sensations because, at a deeper level, we fear to do so will open the gates to pain as well. We're very smart because this is exactly what will happen. *For us to experience pleasure, we must also be willing to risk experiencing pain.* As much as we may try, there is no way to get around this axiom. Morris is an example of someone who learned this lesson the hard way.

Morris unknowingly deadened his pleasure after he lost his wife in a car accident. Jennifer was Morris's second wife and the love of his life. He adored Jennifer. Ten years younger than Morris, Jennifer was beautiful, graceful, loving, sexy, and admiring of Morris's strength. After eleven years of marriage and at age thirty-six, Jennifer was involved in a terrible accident that left her in a coma. She wasted away for over a year before death finally relieved her of her pain. Morris, however, was not relieved of his pain. He was devastated. Watching Jennifer die was the worst pain he had ever known. His feelings of loss, abandonment, frustration, and helplessness were his constant companions while Jennifer was on "death row." These feelings didn't leave him after she died.

I first met Morris two years after Jennifer's death. He had totally isolated himself during the entire two years. A friend had been relentlessly hounding him for months to meet a woman friend of his. Morris, without enthusiasm, finally agreed to a blind date. The woman was stunning. Like Jennifer, she was much younger than Morris. Also like Jennifer, she was graceful, sexy, and admiring of Morris's accomplishments. They dated for six months without any sexual contact. When they finally decided to be sexual with each other, Morris was unable to keep an erection with any consistency. In the beginning, there were times when he seemed just fine. But as the relationship progressed and Morris began to care more and more for this new woman, his erections became less and less.

In our first sessions, Morris talked a great deal about Jennifer. He also spoke about how this new relationship had saved him from his own self-destruction. He was sure he was in love and didn't understand why he was not able to love sexually as well as emotionally. He felt he had finally left the pain of Jennifer's death behind. What he was not consciously aware of was that the pain had lodged itself in his unconscious where it was now masquerading as fear. Like someone burned in a fire for whom fire will always signify pain, Morris's total commitment to another women represented his vulnerability to repeating the pain.

Morris was trying to fool himself into bypassing the fear, but his unconscious stepped in to protect him—in the only way it can. His unconscious communicated to him through his body. If it could talk its message would be, ''You're not ready to commit yet and I won't act as your servant until you deal with your fear. I will not allow you pleasure until you get honest with yourself.''

What Morris needed to do was to be willing to reexperience sorrow and the accompanying feeling of loss and abandonment—not run away from it. His unconscious fear was that he would not survive the pain. Morris needed to be able to image himself as strong enough to pick up the pieces of devastation and to successfully survive the loss of another loving relationship. Not because he could be sure that is what would happen, but because without facing this possibility, he would always be controlled by his unconscious fear of pain—the consequence being his inability to also experience pleasure.

Using visualization, Morris and I worked steadily on images of him being strong enough to endure whatever blows life might give him, including the possibility of losing a third woman. Gradually, Morris began to accept a very unappealing fact. There are no guarantees that what you love won't be taken from you. Instead of living in fear of abandonment, Morris, instead, began to live in the present. He gave up his illusion that he could protect himself by not fully investing in a new relationship. By living in the present, he started experiencing pleasure again and his erections returned.

How Vulnerable Are You? A Personal Test

Because the fear of being able to survive abandonment pain is universal, thinking back on your own losses will help you to determine your vulnerability to fears of abandonment. The more losses you've had, the greater the vulnerability. However, one very traumatic loss is enough to make you very vulnerable. There is no score on this test, but it should give you some insight into your fears of abandonment.

Ask Yourself the Following Questions

1. When I was a child, did I lose a parent or foster parent to death, divorce, or desertion?
2. When I was a child did I lose a grandparent to death or divorce? A sibling?
3. Since childhood, have I lost a parent, grandparent, or sibling?
4. Have I lost any very close friends to death?

5. Have I lost a spouse to death or divorce? How many times?
6. How many long-term intimate sexual relationships have not lasted for me?
7. Have I lost a child to death or marriage?
8. Did I ever lose out to a competitive suitor?
9. Was there lots of sibling rivalry in my family? Did my parents favor a sibling over me?
10. Did I feel really wanted as a child?

The point is that we cannot escape losses. They are a part of living. Sometimes the pain of these losses creates its own illusion—that we won't survive. Think back on a time in your life when you lost someone you really valued. It could be a parent, a lover, or a spouse. At the time, it felt so painful you could hardly get through the day. As time passed, however, the pain did subside and you went on with your life. You did survive the experience. Acknowledging and believing in your strength of survival is what determines your ability to abandon yourself to pleasure without fear of pain.

Use the following visualization to help you to acknowledge your own strength of survival and ability to recover from pain.

* * *

▼

Humpty Dumpty Together Again

Imagine that someone you love has left you. You feel as if your body has been shattered into a hundred pieces that are scattered all over the place. You can't think or make the simplest decisions because you can't get it together. As you look around at the splintered parts of yourself, you feel overwhelmed by the devastation and the pain. You experience being overwhelmed as a draining of all energy and there is no motivation to pick up the pieces. Your fear is that you will never be able to glue the various parts back into their original composition.

Suddenly, in the distance you see a part of yourself you recognize and you know exactly where it goes. With great effort you walk over and pick up the piece and glue it back in place. As you do, you feel a slight increase in energy. Then you see another part of yourself you recognize and you retrieve it and glue it back in place. Your energy is now doubled. You realize that with time and patience you can put all the pieces back together. What you need to do is to glue one piece at a time so that you don't feel overwhelmed by the task. You allow yourself rest periods in between if needed. Slowly, the pieces are forming an image of the original you. As you pick up the last piece and glue it back in place, you realize that you have done such a marvelous job that you can't tell you were ever shattered. You now realize that no matter how devastated you feel by a loss, you will be able to pick up the pieces and carry on. It's not something you volunteer to experience, but it is also not something you fear will permanently destroy you.

▲

Power and Pleasure—
The Oil and Vinegar of Great Sex

For most of us, our images and assumptions associated with power are antithetical to pleasure. Here's why.

- Power means being in control, pleasure means letting go
- Power means self-awareness, pleasure means abandoning self-consciousness
- Power means right versus wrong, pleasure doesn't need losers
- Power means recognition, pleasure doesn't need to discriminate
- Power values strength over weakness, pleasure doesn't know the difference
- Power means being goal oriented, pleasure is a happening

How Needs for Personal Power Interfere with Good Sex

A person who needs to imagine him- or herself as powerful in intimate relationships will find sexual pleasure elusive. Although there are many situations in life where power is appropriate, sexuality is not one of them. Being able to leave power issues outside of the bedroom is not an easy lesson for some. Richard has still not learned how to do this. Instead, his need for power is expressed in a need to control sexual situations.

Richard owns his own company. He's wealthy, commanding, but also very charming. People are attracted to Richard because he gets what he wants in life without being overbearing or rude. Consequently, Richard always seems to have beautiful women on his arm. He was married for many years, although not always faithful. Sex with his wife was never great because Richard had a problem with early ejaculation. Rarely was he able to engage in intercourse for more than a minute without ejaculating. His orgasms were almost always muted, his wife's nonexistent. When his wife divorced him for another man, she told him one reason she was leaving was because he was "a lousy lover."

This was the ultimate in humiliation. Richard was used to success in all aspects of his life. How was it possible that he couldn't get what he wanted sexually? When he started dating after his divorce, he received the last straw in his humiliation: impotency. At first his solution was to abandon whatever woman he was dating and go on to the next. Soon, however, it became obvious to even Richard that he needed some help. That's when I met him.

Richard came to me with the goal of wanting to be able to "perform" in casual sex situations. Several of his male friends seem to be able to do it, why couldn't he? He wasn't interested in marriage at this point in his life and was enjoying dating a variety of women. But the intense embarrassment at his sexual failure was building to a point of paranoia. Richard had never experienced failure. In the past, he had turned failure into success through perseverance and hard work. But with sex, the more he tried, the worse it seemed to get.

Richard's beliefs about sex are typical of many adult males. Their association of male sexuality and masculinity is tied up with images of conquest, achievement, and performance. Some men, like Richard's friends, appear to successfully accomplish the mix. Their performance is well applauded by other similar-thinking males. However, the pleasure they experience is simply the mechanical experience of orgasm. They know little about the rewards of nurturing sensuality. Some men are willing to pay this price in exchange for what to them seems a better payoff: another notch on their belt. Most of them, of course, are simply trying to avoid risking pain by not caring. Others, like Richard, try to imitate the sexual detachment of mechanical pleasure, but are foiled by their bodies.

Just like Morris, Richard's unconscious was speaking to him through his body. What his unconscious was trying to tell him was that he needed to relax during sex, to stop trying to chase pleasure, to let go of needing to perform, and to experience sensations in the moment rather than search for the goal of erection. In other words, Richard must abandon his need to be in control and allow a woman to be in control of his pleasure. This was a risk Richard had never taken.

I worked with Richard on his association of images. It was important for him to be able to blend strength and masculinity with other images than those of being in command. I had him image himself as a kitten being petted. When he did, he said a feeling of being weak came to mind. To him the kitten seemed fragile and helpless. Then I had him image himself as a "king-of-the-jungle" lion being petted. The lion image helped Richard to intellectually understand that he could retain power even though he would be submissive in certain appropriate situations. Sexual pleasure required only that he *temporarily* abandon power.

Even though he was asked to avoid attempting sexual intercourse during therapy, Richard ignored my request. To Richard, avoiding sex felt like avoiding the problem. And Richard was not about to run away from a problem—"only wimps are scared of their shadows." However, in each sexual situation he was unable to relax and receive stimulation. Instinctively he found himself wanting to be in charge rather than being a passive recipient. To do otherwise, made him uncomfortable. He was unable to tolerate the powerless feeling and so he did what he had always done in the past when he felt powerless: He tried to control the situation. Because he was unable to abandon his self-consciousness, his pleasure receptors shut down. He remained impotent.

I asked Richard to visualize a dating situation in which the man felt compelled to impress the woman by taking her to the fanciest, most expensive restaurant in town. So caught up in needing to please the woman, the man is totally preoccupied with whether she is having a good time. His attention is directed toward the service, the food, the temperature, and all other potential roadblocks to a positive experience. He's so concerned about her evaluation that he doesn't even notice his own pleasure. He can't even remember what he had for dinner, much less how it tasted. Richard understood this analogy well. It's what he felt like for years as an early ejaculator.

Eventually, Richard met a woman he really cared for and started dating exclusively. After several weeks, instead of running out on the relationship, he stuck out the awkward and humiliating phase of not getting erections. Once past this phase, he began to relax. His need to perform began to diminish and he started to get erections. Even the problem of early ejaculation disappeared. After two months with this woman he asked her to marry him. She agreed. Two months into their engagement, Richard reversed his decision and broke the engagement. He wasn't ready for marriage, he said. Once again he started dating a variety of women and once again he started having problems with erections.

At this point, Richard quit therapy. The visualizations weren't working with Richard because his fear of sacrificing his masculinity if he stopped being in control kept him from practicing the new images. Until Richard can image a peaceful coexistence between letting go and masculine strength, he will continue to have problems experiencing pleasurable sensations. Impotency will continue to be a part of his life.

How Power Between Two People Interferes with Good Sex

Very few of us like to be told what to do. Even if we don't realize it, being told what to do reminds us of being a child. Back then we were constantly being told what to do: brush your teeth, drink your milk, hurry up, slow down, don't cross the street, get your jacket, kiss Aunt Sally, and on and on. One study indicated the average preschool child receives more than two hundred commands a day. At times, we get rebellious and resist, but it isn't until adolescence that we finally outright rebel. ''You can't tell me what to do!'' we say.

Unfortunately, these early experiences in power control set the stage for future power battles in our relationships. Our ability to successfully work together as a couple depends on how sensitive we are to our early feelings of being told what to do. Depending on how much we had to struggle as a child for our own autonomy, we have either a low, medium, or high degree of tolerance for conflict that generates issues of power. For example, how much control did you have over your choice of dress as a child? Could you wear anything you wanted from an early age or was your choice determined by an adult? What about as a teenager? Did your parents let you set your own style? Think back on your developing years. Did your parents encourage your independent, autonomous thinking and behaving? If not, you might find you have a high need to control others—like you were controlled as a child.

Issues of power often express themselves with couples as a battle for who's right and who's wrong. Being right is a validation of one's self and an offensive position, being wrong then becomes the defensive position. This creates a situation of top dog/underdog in which the underdog feels the need to dig his or her way to the top by virtue of destroying the top dog. The top dog secretly enjoys the power and finds ways to keep the underdog relegated to a defensive position.

Sexual pleasure cannot exist in an environment of conflict between top dog and underdog. As you remember from the chapter on play, we naturally don't feel safe in being vulnerable with our enemies. We must not let our guard down—even in the bedroom—least our enemy take advantage of us. Therefore, we must remain self-conscious and ready to protect ourselves if necessary. Because experiencing pleasurable sensations requires self-abandonment, power struggles between couples destroy sexual pleasure.

Marge and Henry are not unique in their struggle to get along as a couple. Marge is talkative, buoyant, sensitive, emotional, and reactive. Henry is logical, stoic, pensive, and pedantic. Marge and Henry have four children who are each two years apart. There is much chaos in their home. Henry works long hours and leaves Marge to deal with the kids most of the time.

Marge had a very unhappy childhood. She experienced her mother as rigid and cold. Her father was absent most of the time and then died when she was ten. Henry came from a large family of five children. Order was kept in his house by dictatorship. Separately, these two were destined for problems with future power struggles. Together, it was disaster waiting to happen.

Marge is loving, supportive, and devoted to the kids, that is, until her patience is worn thin. Then she is explosive—the pattern of losing her temper and then punishing the children is not uncommon when things get out of control. When Henry gets home late at night, he often finds one or more of the children under some sort of restriction. Sure that Marge has overreacted, he patiently talks with the punished child, explaining and reasoning with them. Sometimes he overrules Marge and takes the child off restriction. Later, after the house has settled down, Henry might approach Marge for sex, only to find a rejecting, angry wife ready for confrontation.

When Marge and Henry came in for counseling, they were going months on end without sexual contact. As was characteristic of them, Marge was tearful and regretful while she told her story; Henry was without emotion and more like an observer rather than a participant in the drama. Henry alluded to his superior parenting skills and subtly boasted about how he was able to get the children to do things whereas Marge's requests always ended in conflict.

Marge was not proud of her reactive nature but still found herself defending her position with the children to Henry. She actually wanted to be more like Henry—more patient and reasonable, but admitting she was wrong was tantamount to being the loser in a battle of wills. Henry's smugness about his style only further infuriated Marge. So she dug her heels in and fought for a position she didn't even believe in.

As long as Marge and Henry remained embattled over a right/wrong strategy, sex between them was bound to be the real loser. It wasn't easy to get these two to come out of the corner and shake hands, but that was the image with which I asked them to work. I had them visualize themselves as a team working toward a common goal, not an enemy that needed to be smashed.

When I asked Marge to visualize her reactive nature

as an animal, the image of a fire-breathing dragon came to mind. No wonder she felt defensive. And no wonder she was unable to control it. She had both empowered it with unconquerable force and labeled it as evil; she was helpless to conquer such a monster. I asked her to switch her visualization from a fire-eating dragon to an ant. She protested at first; she hated her explosiveness and if she stopped hating it, she thought she would never change. I explained that she had to see it as something less formidable or she would always be at an impasse with the dragon. If she didn't hate it so much she could feel less guilty about it being a part of her; controlling it would then be possible.

Henry was asked to visualize himself as flexing his muscles with Marge. Then I asked him what came to mind. He answered, "Marge is at my feet." This image surprised and embarrassed him. He was unaware that he enjoyed having Marge as the underdog. For the first time, he realized that he was unknowingly contributing to Marge's defensiveness because he liked the offensive, controlling position.

When Marge was feeling less guilty about her reactive nature and Henry was beginning to lose the need to take advantage of her guilt, they were on their way to working more as a team rather than as individual players, each seeking to get recognition at the expense of the other. It now seemed possible that Marge could be more vulnerable sexually with Henry—her partner rather than her opponent.

Because all of us have experienced losses in our lives and all of us have the need to feel powerful, it is not easy to abandon self-awareness. The world often seems like a jungle to us, demanding that we constantly be on our toes, always ready to protect ourselves from possible danger. However, like guilt and lust, fear and pleasure cannot coexist. We must be willing to suspend our "radar" if we are to have sexual pleasure. Use the following visualization to help you temporarily surrender power over to pleasure.

The Winds of War . . . and Peace

Imagine yourself as the wind. As the wind you have the power to be quite forceful or quite calm—or any place in between. You chose now to blow with full force and your power is unyielding. You're a force that cannot be ignored. Yet, to keep the force going at full strength requires great expenditures of energy. You want a rest. Suddenly you stop blowing and instead allow a calmness to occur that creates a relaxing peacefulness. You realize that at any time you chose you can regain your power by blowing with force once again. Or you can be moderately forceful, depending on what's needed. But for now you are content to enjoy the serenity created by the calmness. It takes little energy to remain calm and so you are better able to be in touch with your surroundings and to absorb the beauty of what nature has to offer. There is no need to constantly prove your strength because you trust your inherent power and you know it is there waiting for you when you need it.

The Great Balancing Act: Pleasing Yourself versus Pleasing Your Partner

An infant's world is the world of Lilliputians: tiny, help-less, and surrounded by giants who control his or her experience of pleasure and pain. Captive in this world, the infant intuitively knows that pleasing the giants is in his or her best interest. Early in life, we all learn that pleasing is our ticket to survival. At the same time, we are tiny creatures that want immediate gratification. Our entire world is dictated by our senses. We know nothing about patience. We want what we want and we want it now! We scream loudly until we get it.

Juxtapose these two together and we find ourselves balancing on a thin wire our own need for pleasure with our need to please. In the beginning, our innocence tips the scale in favor of our need for immediate gratification. However, as we mature, the juggling of these two op-posing demands intensifies because we now know pa-tience is expected of us. It's not an easy balancing act.

And nowhere is this balance more precarious than in partner sex. There is no other experience in the uni-verse that requires us to *both* be so exquisitely in tune with our own need for pleasure and our need to please at the exact same moment. Lean too far in the direction of self-gratification and you fall into the net of selfish-ness. Lean too far in the direction of pleasing and you lose your ability to experience your own pleasurable sen-sations.

Jan is an example of not being able to balance these two opposing requisites. She is an only child, the daugh-ter of a high-powered politician and socialite mother. Jan was the light of her busy father's life and she has fond memories of being the little girl who jumped up in his lap when he finally came home for the evening. She adored him and loved being able to charm him with her coquettish behavior. From him she could always get what she wanted—as long as she was the sweet, good girl he expected. When she misbehaved, he turned into ice, producing a cold shiver down her spine. Jan learned too well the lesson of how to please.

In her marriage to Robert, Jan unknowingly repeated this pattern. She felt a strong need to be the perfect, loving wife. In return she would be adored by Robert. It felt like a familiar bargain and, for the most part, it worked well. Sexually, however, it created a problem. Jan was not able to orgasm. In fact, she had never had an orgasm with a man. When she came into therapy, she was perplexed by her problem. She was proud of her relationship with Robert and felt her marriage was superior to most. It didn't seem right that she shouldn't also be able to enjoy sex in the way that some of her girlfriends (with less successful marriages) did.

Jan was unaware that what prevented her own pleasure was her excessive need to focus on Robert's pleasure. In fact, she denied that she was trying too hard to please. She saw it differently; she thought she was a great lover—and she had male testimony to prove it. Jan was so accustomed to performing for men, it never occurred to her there was any other way.

Robert, however, had a different story to tell. He felt Jan never completely relaxed during sex. While he was thrilled that Jan was such a generous lover and willing to do anything for him, he wanted to be able to give to her equally. She would not allow it. To him, their lovemaking felt one-sided and this made him feel selfish. Recently, he was noticing that it was becoming more and more difficult for him to become aroused. Jan was surprised to hear Robert's version. She claimed she never heard him say anything like this before. Robert's reply was, "I said it, you just didn't hear it."

Jan still didn't seem convinced. So I sent them home with an assignment. Robert was to spend twenty minutes erotically pleasing Jan. There was to be no intercourse. Jan's job was to do *nothing* but enjoy it and to let any image come freely into her mind. When they returned the next week, Jan was beginning to see the light. She had found it extremely difficult to receive. The whole time Robert was giving to her, she felt compelled to reach out to him. She couldn't stay focused on the pleasurable sensations and didn't even get aroused. Instead, images of icebergs came to mind. The assignment hit home and Jan was now open to working with some very deep beliefs about her need to please and the consequences of not pleasing.

The iceberg, of course, was a vestige of her father's reaction to any expression of her nonpleasing self. To turn this around, we worked first with images of melting the iceberg while Robert was giving to her. Then we worked with images of Robert's enjoyment while he was pleasing Jan. She needed to believe that Robert would still be a loving person if Jan wasn't the pleasing, good girl her father had expected her to be. Slowly, Jan began to feel more comfortable with allowing Robert to give her pleasure. Intercourse was still prohibited, but all other pleasuring was permitted. For the first time in her life, Jan had an orgasm with a man. It was an important breakthrough and led the way for mutual pleasuring with intercourse as well.

If you're having trouble balancing your own pleasure with your need to please, work with the following visualization.

* * *

Dancing As One

You and your partner are on the dance floor, but not yet dancing. The music is playing your favorite slow dance. Rather than assuming that the man will lead, you look into each other's eyes and agree that you'll take turns. You both hold each other around the waist and begin swaying and moving to the music, easily alternating the lead back and forth between you. It doesn't seem to matter that there is no one person in charge. The control flows naturally between the two of you. Without worrying about who's taking charge, you are each free to concentrate on the music and the pleasure it gives you. You're able to tune out all other distractions and focus only on the pleasing melody and the erotic feel of the other person's body. Your bodies start to feel as if they're merging together. Now the two of you are moving as if you are one. As one person, there are no decisions to be made about who is taking the lead. Your bodies glide together, spiraling toward a climax as the music comes to an end.

Pleasure, Play, Lust, and Boredom

Pleasure and play have a lot in common. They both:

- Require abandonment of self-consciousness
- Are spontaneous expressions of the self
- Nurture us so that we are replenished and can keep on going

- Relieve us from the pressures and demands of life
- Keep boredom from setting in

Those of us who know how to truly play also know how to experience pleasure. The two go hand-in-hand together. When they are joined by lust, great sex happens. These three companions, play, pleasure, and lust, are what give meaning to our lives. They allow us to keep investing in life, in spite of difficulties, setbacks, painful losses, or failures.

Sex loses its luster when we let these three companions slip from our lives. All three are right-brain functions and we need to expend energy to keep them alive in a world that demands mostly left-brain activity. Visualization is an effective way to help you keep these three companions in the forefront of your life.

► CHAPTER *8*

What's Love Got to Do with It?

▼

Feeling Loved Is What Counts

I think of love as being connected to sex in a slightly different way than most. What seems to be essential to really great sex is not the state of love but the state of *feeling* loved. Feeling loved is synonymous with feeling safe. When we feel loved, we feel both respected for who we are and free from fears of abandonment. Feeling respected and no longer fearing abandonment, we feel less vulnerable to hurt and can then freely give and receive intimate touch, lust, play, and pleasure, the essential elements to really great, long-lasting, satisfying sex.

The state of feeling loved is not static. In any relationship, feeling loved fluctuates with the relationship's natural ups and downs. If we've had a recent fight, for example, we may feel less loved and, therefore, less safe about our fears of abandonment. Most of us are unaware that we're feeling unsafe. We are aware, however, that we don't feel sexual. When couples come to me for therapy, they have zeroed in on sex as the problem. Sexual problems are tangible. They can be observed. An unsafe feeling is abstract and much more difficult to articulate.

It's difficult to give or receive sex during a time when we are feeling unsafe or insecure. Consequently, sexual desire waxes and wanes, depending on how safe we feel about being loved. In the following case, the appearance of an old girlfriend created an unsafe feeling and then a loss of sexual desire.

Justine came to me in tears. She had no sexual desire for her husband and was desperate to regain even a small amount of sexual passion. Yet, each time he approached her she found herself unable to even minimally respond. In her previous relationships she was overwhelmingly passionate. She knew she had it in her, but she couldn't figure out what was wrong with her now. Because her husband still felt sexual desire for her, Justine was convinced that it was her problem—not his.

Until we reviewed in detail the recent events in her life, Justine remained confused about her lack of sexual response. Using visualization, I asked Justine to image a wall in front of her. The wall was to represent the sexual block she was feeling. Then I asked her to image a picture on the wall and to tell me what she saw. What came to mind was the face of a woman. At first Justine couldn't identify her, but as she concentrated she realized that the woman was both an old girlfriend and a colleague of her husband. The woman had recently returned to the area after having lived abroad for several years. Once again, the woman and her husband were working together.

Until this visualization, Justine thought she had resolved her jealousy over this woman. It hadn't even occurred to her that the woman could have anything to do with her lack of sexual desire toward her husband. Her reappearance had created feelings of insecurity and caused Justine to question her husband's love for her. Unknowingly, her fears of abandonment kicked in and cut off her sexual desire.

Once Justine realized what was inhibiting her sexual desire, she could talk to her husband about it. With his reassurance that he was no longer interested in his former girlfriend, Justine started to feel secure again in his love and her sexual desires began to return.

Active versus Passive: Falling in Love versus Staying in Love

Falling in love is something that happens *to* us. Staying in love is something we must *make* happen. One is passive and the other, active. Love asks a great deal of us. It takes tremendous energy to continually accept and respect another person. Because they are imperfect, our partners will, inevitably at times, disappoint us, frustrate us, anger us, and even reject us. In order to stay in love, we must be willing to forgive our partner for not always being exactly who we want them to be. We also must be able to keep giving even though things may not always go smoothly. In turn, we need our partner to do the same for us.

Think of love as money in a bank. If each partner puts "love money" in the bank each day, no matter how difficult it seems at the time, the account will grow steadily. When times are rough, there will be a cushion to draw on. If each partner, however, waits for the other one to put love money in before matching it, the account will grow slowly or not at all. During troubled times there will be no reserves.

Common Relationship Problems— Is This a Description of You?

Using visualizations can help us be more giving and forgiving. It's possible, with the aid of visualizations, to more quickly turn a negative situation into a positive one.

Imagery helps us to get a different perspective on whatever problem we're struggling with at the time. Listed below are some very common relationship problems. *All of these problems keep us from feeling safe and, therefore, interfere with satisfying sex.* Following each is a visualization that helps us to be more forgiving.

If you find yourself blocking or unable to use the visualizations listed below, it's possibly a sign that your relationship is not on steady enough grounds to be able to keep giving or to forgive. Or it's possible that forgiving is not the appropriate thing to do. Read the next sections to see what you might do about this.

Power Struggles

As discussed in chapter 7, pleasurable sex is virtually impossible between two people who are engaged in a contest for power. It's impossible to be dueling for recognition and respect and to feel loved at the same time. Try this visualization to lessen any power struggles you might have with your partner.

* * *

The Tug-of-War

Imagine you and your partner on opposite sides of a line. You both are tugging on the ends of a rope, trying to get the other one to cross the line to your own side. You're both pulling with all your strength. It takes tremendous energy to keep pulling on the rope, but you know if you weaken, you'll end up being pulled across the line. Then, you'll be the loser.

Suddenly, you begin to question why you want so strongly to stay on your side of the line. It doesn't look more desirable than what's on the other side. Besides, you already know what your side looks like. It occurs to you that you might learn something about yourself and your partner if you're willing to investigate what's on the other side.

You realize that the struggle is not about the best place to be, but who wins. Then it occurs to you that there may be a price to pay for being the winner. What will you do with a partner whose been forced to come over to your side? Will it feel all that good? Will you really be the winner?

Gently, you stop pulling on the rope. Instead, you voluntarily walk over to the other side. Now you're not only physically but emotionally on the same side as your partner. Things look very different from this perspective. You feel somehow enlarged, even wiser, by seeing the new perspective. You also feel more energy now that you're no longer pulling against something. What you notice is that by not needing to be the winner, you actually feel like one.

Partners as Parents

To some extent, we all make parents of our partners. Without being aware of it, we turn male partners into fathers we expect to take care of us and female partners into mothers who make unrealistic demands on us. To some degree we all do it. It's human nature. If it's not carried to extremes, we manage to keep these feelings from interfering in a major way. However, this tendency can create both severe relationship and sexual problems. If our need to reestablish childhood issues of authority or dependency are especially strong, we will be unable to be sexual with our partners. When partners establish too strong a parent-child relationship, it evokes the incest taboo, shutting down sexual responses.

This is exactly what happened to Sherry and Greg. Sherry is an exceptionally bright and organized person. She manages the household, takes the principal responsibility for their two toddlers, and works full time in her own public relations firm. Greg is an attractive but quiet person. He makes an excellent living as a plumber and is very skilled in his field.

Sherry feels continually turned off to Greg in spite of the fact that she still thinks Greg is the most attractive man she knows. When Greg approaches her for sex, she feels herself go "completely cold." In the initial therapy session, she wondered if perhaps it was because she wished Greg would do more to help with the children. Was she punishing him for not being more helpful?

When asked to visualize and focus on Greg when he approached her sexually, the image that came to mind was that of a shy little boy. The visualization helped Sherry to recognize that it was her interpretation of his behavior as childlike that made her go cold. Getting turned on to a little boy was simply unthinkable.

With these issues out in the open, it became possible

for Sherry and Greg to modify their behavior. Greg worked with visualizations that imaged himself as stronger and more assertive in all areas of his life. Sexually, he worked with approaching Sherry in a more direct, "adult" fashion. At the same time, Sherry worked with images of seeing Greg as more adult. It took some time for the incest taboo to fade. Change is rarely immediate. Over several months, however, Sherry found herself warming up to Greg's new approach and sex once again became a part of their lives.

Defensive Communication

Unless we've studied debate or speech, few of us give much consideration to *how* we phrase what we say. Our patterns of communication come automatically. In fact, thinking about how we are saying something feels very awkward.

There is, however, an art and science to successful communication. Certain styles of relating either engender understanding between people or engender defensive responses that prohibit understanding. When one partner has an offensive communication style, it tends to create a defensive position in the other. It takes effort to avoid falling into this trap. If both partners have a tendency to communicate defensively, it takes even greater effort to stop the circular process. The circular process can only be broken when one partner is willing to be the first to risk being vulnerable. The remaining partner no longer has an opponent.

If you feel like you're defending yourself too much and need to be constantly on guard with your partner, try the following visualization to lessen this feeling.

* * *

Letting Down Your Guard

Imagine that you are in a boxing ring with your partner. You're both wearing boxing gloves. You're circling each other, not sure when the first punch will come. It all feels very familiar because you've been in this boxing ring hundreds of times. Sometimes you've been the one to walk away with a knockout, sometimes you've been the one left flat on the mat. One thing you know for certain, is that you can't let your guard down for even a second. If you do, whammo!

It feels exhausting to be constantly on guard. Knocking down the enemy takes energy, so does defending yourself. You're feeling tired and what you really want is to be someplace else where it feels safe. You start to wonder what would happen if you stayed in the ring, but took off the boxing gloves. Would your partner still consider you an opponent if you stopped defending yourself? Do you dare risk finding out? If you don't risk it, you'll continually be drained by the energy it takes to defend yourself. You decide it's worth the risk.

You take off your gloves and allow yourself to become totally vulnerable by facing your partner head on without a defense. Your partner is completely disarmed. It becomes clear there is no need to spar with a defenseless partner. Your partner takes off his or her gloves and reaches out to shake your hand.

Nondefensive Communication

Studies in interpersonal communication have found certain styles of communication to promote either supportive or defensive behaviors. Defensive styles tend to make a person feel under attack and they will automatically respond by defending themselves. Listening becomes impossible under these circumstances. Supportive styles, on the other hand, tend to make a person feel accepted and, therefore, promote both listening and understanding.

Behaviors that tend to create defensiveness include:

> *Evaluation:* Sender seems to be evaluating or judging the listener.
> EXAMPLE: ''You always or never . . .''
> *Control:* Sender is intending to change an attitude, influence behavior, or restrict behavior.
> EXAMPLE: ''Why don't you . . .''
> *Superiority:* Sender conveys a superior position.
> EXAMPLE: ''I could have told you that.''
> *Certainty:* Sender wants to win rather than negotiate.
> EXAMPLE: ''It's always worked for me.''

Behaviors that tend to be supportive include

> *Description:* Sender requests or gives information.
> EXAMPLE: ''I've noticed . . .''
> *Problem Orientation:* Sender communicates a desire to collaborate.
> EXAMPLE: ''Why don't we consider . . .''

> *Equality:* Sender communicates equal status.
> EXAMPLE: Using ''we'' instead of ''you.''
> *Provisionalism:* Sender gives message of willing-
> ness to experiment.
> EXAMPLE: ''Let's try . . .''

Finding Fault

In new relationships we are very forgiving. We even find certain shortcomings ''cute.'' It's certainly true that in the beginning ''love is blind.'' During the period known as falling in love, we *automatically* operate in our right brain. Passion prevails, blocking out our more critical side. However, day-to-day exposure to human imperfection tends to chip away at passion. The idiosyncrasies and faults we either didn't see or forgave sometimes become all-consuming. In long-term relationships, our ability to be forgiving is challenged every single day. Depending on how we deal with this challenge, we either stay in love or let love die.

If we're unable to be forgiving, we begin to focus on our partner's faults. Little things start to get on our nerves. We feel guilty about being so picky over such inconsequential things. Our guilt makes us try to snuff out critical feelings. Soon, like a pressure cooker, we explode over some insignificant behavior. Our explosion increases our guilt so we try harder to be more patient. The cycle starts all over again. Loving feelings are severely burdened under these circumstances.

The solution comes with learning how to forgive. Instead of looking outside ourselves we, need to begin with self-forgiveness. We have to forgive our own imperfections before we can forgive others. It sounds too simple to work, but it does. When we release the pressure on ourselves to be perfect, when we treat our weaknesses as friends, not enemies, we have the energy and strength to stay focused on the positive aspects of our partners. The negative ones don't go away, but they don't seem so intolerable.

Try this visualization and you'll see what I mean.

▼

Mistaken Indemnity

You've just received a notice in the mail that you bounced a check. You immediately get angry. It can't be possible you say. The bank must have made an error. You're very careful about not letting such things happen. You always check and recheck your balance to be sure this doesn't happen. You feel the tension rising in your body as you think about the inconvenience of correcting the mistake. You have to make a trip to the bank, call the company you wrote the check to, rewrite the check, and so on.

You go get your checkbook to see where the bank might have made an error. As you go over the figures, you discover the error was yours. How could it be? You recalculate, but get the same result. How could you be so stupid you ask yourself. What a careless thing to do. You spend several minutes being critical of your mistake. Finally, you leave it alone and go on with something else.

You think you've forgotten all about it. Later that day you're searching for something and can't find it. You just know your partner has once again put something where you can't find it. You yell at your partner, "Where did you put . . . ?" Soon the two of you are fighting.

▲

Now try replaying this scene and notice the difference in the possible outcome.

▼

Instant Replay

You just received a notice in the mail that you bounced a check. Strange, you say. You don't usually do that. Perhaps you were careless this time. You check your checkbook and locate the error. You look at your schedule to find some time to correct the problem. Then you go on to other things.

Later that day you're searching for something you can't find. You know how your partner dislikes things laying around. Maybe he or she put it away. You ask your partner, "I can't seem to find. . . . Do you remember seeing it?" Later the two of you are having sex.

▲

Boredom

From chapter 1 you will recall that boredom results from a feeling of uninvolvement. It inevitably happens when we spend too much time in routine, analytic activities that fail to challenge our creative selves or activate our playful nature. From chapter 6 you'll recall that so many of our everyday activities fail to challenge either of these two parts of us.

Adding to the problem, is the fact that human beings have a tendency to gravitate toward repetitive patterns. Habits or patterns require less energy and seem to make life simpler. Without a concerted effort to prevent it, sex, like other activities, tends toward a repetitive pattern. The problem is that a natural consequence of the routine is a feeling of uninvolvement; boredom soon follows. It's another one of the many circular processes.

This circular process is made more complex by the frequent inclination to blame our partners for sexual boredom. We want someone else to create the excitement. By making it their fault we avoid taking responsibility for our own lack of energy. Apparently, we never outgrow the childhood propensity for deflecting blame: "He started it," "She made me do it," or "It wasn't my fault."

The only way to alleviate boredom is to counteract it with an investment of our own energy. Rather than pointing the finger at our partner's lack of investment, we need to take action to change the situation. This takes energy. Use the following visualization to help you get the necessary energy to reinvest in your sex life.

* * *

185

A Whiff of Creative Energy

Imagine that in your bedroom you have a large tank, much like an oxygen tank. Inside the tank is stored creative energy. It's an odorless, colorless gas. There is a tube connected to the tank and at the end of the tube is a small mask. Each morning before you get out of bed you turn on the tank and breathe in through the mask a small amount of the gas. Seconds after you breathe in the gas you begin to feel a change in your energy level. You feel rested from a good sleep plus charged with an extra dose of creativity. After taking a whiff of the gas, you lie in bed for a few minutes longer, letting your thoughts wander toward erotic ways to revitalize your sex life. The thoughts come without much effort. You begin to look forward to the next sexual encounter so you can put some of your ideas into action.

Lack of Trust

In personal relationships, trust is equated with freedom from fears of abandonment. As discussed in chapter 7, if we've experienced a traumatic loss or a series of losses, we may have difficulty believing we can trust no matter how trustworthy our partners prove to be. More likely, however, is the problem of broken trust caused by a severed sexual-exclusivity contract. When trust has been damaged, our fears of abandonment are brought to the surface. Sexual pleasure almost always suffers because we no longer feel safe.

Once trust is damaged, there are no easy ways to repair it. To regain trust we must be willing to reinvest our emotions without a guarantee we won't be hurt again. It's an act of faith, not in another person, but in our own ability to survive. Only then can we feel safe enough to be vulnerable again.

This was what Karen discovered in dealing with her husband's affair. At first she was so torn apart she didn't believe she could go on with her life. All the previous losses in her life came bubbling to the surface. Her father had suffered a stroke when she was a small child. He lived, but was without full mental capacity and Karen felt she never had a father like other children. She also felt her mother had favored her sister and the pain around this issue began to emerge. Her hysterectomy at age twenty-two meant she would never bear children. She thought she had dealt with her forced childlessness until she discovered the affair, when, she was flooded with feelings of loss for the children she would never have.

Karen didn't want to end her marriage and she knew her total lack of interest in sex had been contributory to her husband's affair. Karen worked with the "Humpty Dumpty" visualization of putting the torn pieces of herself back together again, this time with greater strength. As she began to trust her ability to survive losses, she turned her attention to the issues of her low sexual desire and his affair. Both seemed so much easier to confront once she realized she could cope with whatever losses might come her way. It took over a year of couple therapy before Karen felt safe enough to be comfortably sexual with her husband. She forgave him because she wanted to move on with her life and abandon living in fear of abandonment.

If you're having trouble trusting someone you want to be close to, try the following visualization.

A Leap of Faith

You're standing at the edge of a cliff. The drop-off is several hundred feet down. You need to get across to the cliff on the opposite side of the crevice. The distance between the two cliffs is about three feet. On the opposite side is someone you deeply care about. The person is holding out his or her hand and telling you to jump. He or she tells you it will be okay because he or she will not let you fall. You keep looking at the person, trying to decide if you can trust him or her. Can the person really ensure your safety? Should you take a leap of faith?

Suddenly, you realize that he or she can't guarantee you won't be hurt. Instead of trying to decide if the person is trustworthy, you begin to think about your own capability for making the crossing. As you study the distance, you begin to feel a confidence in your own strength. You decide you can go the distance on your own. The leap of faith is in yourself. Trusting yourself, you don't need to trust the other person. You easily make the jump. Now you're with the person you want to be with and you made it happen because of the belief in your own strength to survive.

Not Being Able to Receive

Those of us who carry around a lot of guilt have a difficult time receiving from others. We're not born feeling guilty. We come into the world with a love of self. Guilt is imposed on us by well-intended but misguided adults, usually parents or the church. Sometimes guilt attaches itself to us as the result of circumstances beyond our control such as physical or sexual abuse.

When we have a lot of guilt, compliments and gifts make us uncomfortable. Love, which is one kind of gift, is also difficult to receive. We allow little pleasure in our lives, especially sexual pleasure. Participation in sex is out of obligation, a desire to be "normal," or a desire to get attention, but there is little sexual satisfaction. As a result, sexual desire is usually low. We don't complain, though, because we don't deserve any better—low self-esteem always accompanies guilt.

Guilt and low self-esteem create yet another circular process. To rid ourselves of the guilt we have to feel worthy of happiness. The low self-esteem keeps us from feeling deserving so we hang on to the guilt as a punishment for being an unworthy person. Round and round it goes. The cycle causes us to unintentionally sabotage the good thing in our lives.

Cindy is just such a person. Cindy is strikingly beautiful and intelligent. She, however, thinks she's a loser. Cindy was sexually abused by her father. Her mother was extremely religious and made sure that Cindy was taught right from wrong. Sex was a definite "wrong." Not surprisingly, sex was very problematic for Cindy. The confusing messages created an unrelenting conflict. If sex was wrong, why did her father want her to do it? In Cindy's eyes, her parents could never be the problem so it could only be there was something wrong with her. As a young teenager and later, as an adult, she used sex in all the wrong ways: to get attention, to please a man, and to keep from being abandoned. Even though she had lots of sex, she couldn't care less about it and she never had orgasms.

Once she went away for the weekend with her boyfriend. She had a wonderful sexual experience in which she felt pleasure for the first time. She lay awake all night feeling terribly guilty. Somehow she felt she would be punished for enjoying herself. When asked to visualize her guilt she described it as a ball and chain that she constantly carried with her. As her visualization assignment, I asked her to imagine reaching down and opening the lock on the chain.

When she returned the next week, she said she could see herself trying to unlock the chain, but she couldn't get the lock to open. Cindy's imagery indicated she wasn't ready to let go of her guilt. She still needed it to drag her down—where she deserved to be. I asked her what it would take to feel deserving of happiness and she said, "To be born again to different parents."

We began working with visualizations centered around rebirth. Cindy created a scene where she was born again—this time into a world that was loving and gentle and without emotional conflict. She imaged herself as a happy, carefree child with loving parents. These visualizations gave Cindy her first look at the possibility of a different type of life. A life that allowed her to be a good child, not the evil child she always felt herself to be. As a good child, she deserved happiness and she deserved pleasure. It took many months of constant work with these visualizations for Cindy to begin to think differently about herself.

Then we tried working again with images of unlocking the ball and chain. This time Cindy could see herself successfully getting the lock undone. Gradually she began to stop sabotaging her own sexual pleasure. Once she was able to experience pleasure without guilt, she moved to images of letting go of control during intercourse. Finally, after more than two years of therapy, Cindy was able to orgasm during sex.

Problems That Don't Go Away— Or When to Throw In the Towel

When We Shouldn't Forgive

While forgiveness is necessary for long-lasting love, it should not be totally unconditional. There are certain circumstances or behaviors that should not be forgiven. A husband who continually beats his wife or a wife who repeatedly is unfaithful are only two examples. Forgiveness needs to be circumstantial, not global. There are no blanket rules that work in every case.

Just about the only useful guideline that I've found over the years is one that has to do with patterns of behavior. Patterns are very resistant to change and, therefore, provide clues to future predictions of behavior. Unfortunately, patterns are not that easy to determine. If a person has cheated twenty times—that's a pattern. He or she is very likely to do it again. But what if they've only cheated twice? Is that a pattern?

The field of psychology is concerned with the study of human behavior in the attempt to determine predictive behaviors that establish patterns. For example, sexual molestation of a child indicates a distortion of erotic association that is very resistant to change. Such behavior has been labeled compulsive; it's not under the voluntary control of the person. Forgiving a partner for a compulsive behavior is not wise because it will happen again and again.

It's best to seek professional help whenever there is a question of compulsive behavior. Professional help is also extremely useful when there is a question about the appropriateness of when to forgive. As mentioned, professionals can't give you blanket rules, but they can help you understand predictive human behavior and they can help you understand yourself.

For example, a woman came to me wanting to know if she should forgive her husband for his ten-year rejection of her in favor of daily masturbation. She wanted to know if his masturbation was compulsive. I, on the other hand, wanted to know why she had been waiting ten years to ask the question. Therapy was directed at helping her answer that question.

Choosing the Wrong Partner

There's nothing more complex than the human process of partner selection. Without asking it to, our unconscious has significant participation in the decision. Sometimes it causes us to make choices that are totally wrong for us. For example, we all know people who marry on the rebound only to find it is a mistake. One such client of mine ended up in a miserable situation. She came into therapy in a distraught state. Her boyfriend of two years had ended their relationship. Having failed at a previous marriage, she was desperate to make this one work. She convinced herself that he didn't really mean what he said. She tried relentlessly to get him back—to no avail.

One night while out on the town, she met a man in a singles bar. Against my advice, she married three months later and, simultaneously, dropped out of therapy. In less than a year she was back in my office. She was in terrible pain over the marriage. On their honeymoon she discovered he had an uncontrollable temper. Since then she experienced extreme verbal abuse from him daily. She asked me if I would see them as a couple. I agreed to meet with them.

When he walked into the office I did a double take—he was a physical clone of her previous boyfriend. Based on her strong need to reunite with her boyfriend, she unconsciously tried to resurrect him through another man. She didn't even take the time to find out who this new man really was. She made her choice for the wrong reason. Therapy could not change that. I did not offer them marital counseling but I did offer to work with her to face her mistake and separate. She declined, preferring instead to deny his *pattern* of abuse and to find excuses for his anger.

There is no specific sign that tells us when we've made a wrong choice in partners. People are not perfect so relationships are not perfect. All relationships will have some problems. These problems should be offset, however, by some good times. Visualize yourself graphing your relationship. The good times are at the top of the graph, the not-so-good times at the bottom. If the line of the graph looks like a small wave, you're probably like most of us. If the line has high peaks, countered by very low points, you have a conflict that needs to be explored. If the graph line started out high and goes straight down, you definitely need to seek some professional help.

When the Physical Attraction Is Gone

Physical attraction is a significant part of sexuality. Standards of physical beauty are universal, existing in all cultures throughout history. Also universal is the custom of associating these standards of beauty with eroticism. This is done through cultural rituals. In western culture, these rituals are subtle rather than obvious as in more primitive cultures. In primitive cultures there might be an erotic ritual dance that celebrates beauty. In the western world, it is done through imagery as in paintings or, now, as in movies, magazines, and advertising. It's usually so subtle that we may not know exactly how we developed our physical ideal. Just the same, as adults we all emerge with some standard of what is attractive to us and what turns us on.

There are some of us whose eroticism is strongly

tied to narrow standards of imagery. Unless a partner "fits" that standard, we may not be able to be aroused. Sometimes a change in body image may kill eroticism. I remember a short-term patient who claimed to be totally turned off to his wife because she gained five pounds over what he considered to be acceptable. He refused to consider that his standards were unrealistic. Instead, he constantly monitored her eating, commenting on just about any "fattening" food she bought at the grocery store or ordered in a restaurant.

Although this is an extreme example, we all have some notion of what is attractive to us. Some of us are more flexible about our eroticism and imagery than others. If we tend to be inflexible, we find that we're not as easily erotically influenced by anything except physical factors. We're not likely, for example, to overlook body image in favor of personality characteristics. If we're inflexible, we usually, but not always, have fairly rigid standards for ourselves as well. This helps us to feel legitimate about our standards. Our thinking may be, "I stay in shape—why can't he or she?"

I am frequently asked whether there can be good sex without physical attraction. It's a complicated question because it involves the issue of flexibility. The more flexible, the less important physical beauty is to a our eroticism. So, the answer becomes, some of us can and some of us can't, depending on how attached we are to our standards.

Working with visualizations can expand our flexibility in regard to physical beauty, but we have to be flexible enough to be willing to try and motivated enough to practice the visualizations. My record with rekindling eroticism when the physical attraction has disappeared (or was never really there) is not good. Inflexible people are rarely open to expanding their visual attachments to eroticism. Instead, they attempt to change their environment rather than themselves. It seems easier to look for a new partner or even to go without sex than to work with changing their erotic attachments.

When Only One Is Doing All the Giving and Forgiving

Using visualization to become a more giving and forgiving person helps us to have more satisfying relationships. However, it won't work if only one of us is doing all of the giving and forgiving. At some point, which is really definable only by circumstances, we must feel we're getting something back in return. If we've reached the point where we're mentally keeping a ledger on who's giving or forgiving, it's a sign of trouble. Once we've reached that point we're already in a tug-of-war. It's a perfect time for *both* partners to get back on track by using the "Tug-of-War" visualization.

A successful relationship is based not on commonality but on mutuality. We don't have to be the same or do the same things for each other, but we do have to feel mutual respect. One-way giving and forgiving never works over the long run. That's because we're humans, not saints. When we don't receive in return, we don't feel loved; trouble is just around the corner.

Making Love in Public—Do You Dare?

Feeling loved is very much connected to the little everyday expressions of caring. These expressions originate in the right brain. Some examples are a spontaneous telephone call to tell someone you're thinking about them, a greeting card with a loving message that arrives without a special occasion, a hand reaching across a table when you're out in public, and a true greeting of appreciation at the beginning or ending of the day. These and other expressions that are considered to be romantic are right-brain activities and serve to stoke the embers of passion, readying them for the flames necessary for passionate sex. If you don't continually stoke the fire, it becomes difficult to get the flames going when you want to turn up the heat.

Romance is not just an idealistic notion relegated to poets or to new lovers. Being a right-brain activity, romance stimulates the senses, engages our playful and lustful side, leads us to pleasure, and makes us feel loved. These are all the ingredients needed for long-lasting, satisfying sex.

CHAPTER 9

Using Visualization to Solve Specific Sexual Problems

▼

The preceding chapters dealt with the requisites for sexual satisfaction: concentration, intimate touch, masturbation, lust, play, pleasure, and feeling loved. In this chapter, you can get a closer look at how these core issues of sexuality are important in eliminating specific sexual problems. The problems addressed—which included orgasm difficulty, erection difficulty, and premature ejaculation—are those that are most common in the general population.

Each of these sexual problems has three stages:

1. The trigger or cause
2. Inability to concentrate on pleasure
3. Symptoms

The three stages operate in varying degrees of conscious awareness, with each producing the next level. Here's how it might work with the symptom of orgasm difficulty.

Something out of our awareness, the trigger, results in our being unable to stay focused on erotic pleasure. The interruption of concentration produces the symptom, in this case difficulty with orgasm. We have awareness at the symptom level but we may or may not be aware of our focusing problem. What started the whole process—the unconscious cause—could, for example, be shame about feelings of lust.

In most cases, it's necessary to remove the underlying cause in order to be able to focus on erotic pleasure. The visualizations in the previous chapters are designed to remove the deeper causes of the inability to stay focused. However, if you've been having a specific sexual symptom, it's natural to want to try to zero in on a specific solution without exploring the more remote cause.

A word of advice: No matter what the symptom, eliminating it requires the ability to concentrate on pleasure so be sure you're familiar with the concepts discussed in chapter 7 before you continue reading. If you skip that chapter, you'll be sabotaging any efforts to change.

If you've picked up this book to look for a shortcut to your particular problem, you may also look for shortcuts in sex. If this is true about you, it may give you a clue as to why you have difficulty concentrating: You're looking ahead instead of experiencing pleasure in the moment. Be honest with yourself. If you tend to go for shortcuts, resist the temptation in this case. It's the only way you'll benefit from this book.

Orgasms Too Soon, Orgasms Too Late, or Possibly Erections That Won't Cooperate— Are They Possible to Eliminate?

Sexual Symptoms: The Human Sexual Response Cycle

What I've labeled as symptoms are any problems that interfere with the natural flow of the human sexual response cycle. During sexual arousal our bodies go through a predictable physiological response. The phases of this cycle have been named by researchers Masters and Johnson as excitement, plateau, orgasm, and resolution.

Excitement. During the excitement phase, the body prepares itself for arousal by an increase in heart and respiration rate and a dilation of vessels in the genitals. The blood flows to the genitals causing erections in males and swelling and lubrication in females. Changes also occur in the breasts and there is a general response called the sex flush, resulting from the increased blood flow to all parts of the body.

Plateau. During the plateau phase, there is a leveling off of sexual tension. The body is fully aroused but seems to pause, as if to gain maximum anticipatory pleasure before moving on to the orgasm phase. The amount of time involved in the plateau phase varies considerably among individuals and from one sexual situation to another.

Orgasm. Exactly what triggers the orgasm phase is unknown. It seems to be an extremely complex interaction of physical, emotional, social, hormonal, and perhaps some other unknown factors. During the orgasm phase, there are strong muscular contractions in the genital area that actually push the congested blood out, causing the pleasurable sensations and tension release. In most men, ejaculation occurs simultaneously with orgasm.

Resolution. The resolution phase follows orgasm. In both men and women the resolution phase is a period of return to normal. Heart rate and respiration decrease and blood flow returns to the prearousal state. Genital swelling, breast changes, and the sex flush disappear. In most men, resolution immediately follows orgasm and there is a mandatory refractory period before arousal may occur again. The time of the refractory period varies from man to man and increases with age. In women, resolution may be postponed by continued sexual stimulation so that repeated orgasms are possible.

Common Sexual Symptoms

The most common sexual symptoms are:

- Problems with the excitement phase, experienced as the symptom of erection difficulties in men; lubrication and swelling difficulties in women.
- Problems with the plateau phase, experienced as the symptom of premature orgasm in both men and women
- Problems with the orgasm phase, experienced as the symptom of delayed or nonexistent orgasm in men and women

Problems with the Excitement Phase: Causes and Solutions

Erection Difficulties in Males

Physical. Many erection difficulties may be physical in nature. There are some illnesses and medical conditions that impair erections, especially as a man ages. Prescription and recreational drugs, including alcohol, also can physiologically impair erection. If erections are impaired in all situations, including masturbation and in the early morning, a man should consult a physician who specializes in the diagnosis of sexual dysfunctions to determine if impairment is physical or psychological.

Psychological. Loss of concentration is the effect of all problems, in which a man is physically capable of attaining erection but is psychologically blocking arousal. Instead of focusing on pleasurable sensations, the man is distracted. Distraction can result from many different causes, acting independently or in combination. These different causes can be grouped, however, into some principal categories. These are

- Fear of psychological pain, which blocks pleasure (see chapter 7)
- Inability to balance own pleasure with needing to please and perform (see chapter 7)
- Feelings of guilt and shame surrounding lust and/or pleasure (see chapters 5 and 7)
- Fear of failure as a result of a previous failure
- Inappropriate or ineffective sexual stimulation (see chapter 9)
- Not wanting to be there in the first place (see chapter 9)

Because all deeper causes of erection problems have the end result of concentration loss, resolutions require restoring the ability to concentrate. Erections are an involuntary response to appropriate sexual stimuli. When a man is relaxed and focused on the pleasurable sensations received during stimulation, the involuntary response occurs naturally. However, if he is unable to focus on the pleasure of the moment, the erection reflex will not occur. Further explanation of the momentary nature of pleasure is described in chapter 7.

An analogy helps explain how the reflex may be impaired. Visualize a baseball player at bat. The essential ingredient is concentration—watching the ball being pitched. If the batter is distracted in the slightest, his concentration is destroyed. He can't be thinking about striking out, about tomorrow's game or yesterday's game, or about impressing his girlfriend in the stands *and* be concentrating on watching the ball at the same time. Each of these thoughts takes him away from the immediate task of watching the ball, concentration is lost and the ball goes past him. If concentration is lost during sex, the sensations go past a man and he "strikes out."

Once a man has experienced striking out, he falls into a trap of self-fullfilling performance anxiety. He begins to anticipate possible failure and thus ensures his inability to concentrate. We are familiar with performance anxiety in athletes when even the best of athletes "choke" under pressure. Anxiety affects sexual performance in the same way. The only difference is the way in which the anxiety is experienced.

Most men don't even realize they are anxious. That's because they are looking for more "typical" signs of anxiety such as increased heart rate or the familiar pit-in-the-stomach type of anxiety. Sexual anxiety, however, is experienced as a different sort of physiological response—an interference with the arousal phase. Because many men fail to interpret erection failure as a signal of anxiety, they don't identify themselves as anxious. They remain puzzled, frustrated, humiliated, confused, and impotent.

What men don't understand is they unknowingly sabotage their own sexual performance by monitoring their erections. In doing so, they induce anxiety into the sexual situation and prohibit themselves from experiencing the pleasure of the immediate moment. Anxiety and pleasure cannot physiologically exist at the same time. Like lust and guilt, anxiety and pleasure operate in an either/or type fashion. Refer to chapter 5 for a more detailed discussion of the mutual exclusiveness of two opposing emotions.

The solution at the symptom level is to regain concentration. Visualization is a technique that has been used for several decades in athletics to help athletes restore concentration. In the 1984 Olympics, terms such as *inner calm, achieving flow, programming the subconscious,* and *visual imagery* became familiar. These techniques, which make up the experience of visualization (see chapter 1), have proven effective in helping to regain concentration.

Use the following visualization to help regain your ability to concentrate ''in the moment.''

▼

Alone in the Crowd

You are a star basketball player involved in an important play-off game. The score is tied and there are only two seconds left to play. You're at the free-throw line. The outcome is in your hands and your ability to concentrate on getting the ball in the basket. The crowd is going wild, stomping their feet and shouting out your name over and over again. You know you must block out all distractions. It must be just you and the basket. You totally forget about winning or losing. Everyone around you fades away. There is complete silence. The intensity of your concentration allows you to erase everything from your mind except the basket. Now it's just you and the basket. With your intense concentration you have made the distance between you and the basket seem to disappear. Now you're as one with the basket. There is no anxiety and no insecurity about the outcome; you simply reach out and drop in the ball. As soon as you do, the crowd around you comes back into focus. They're on their feet calling out your name. The buzzer goes off, signaling the end of the game. Your teammates surround you, lift you on their shoulders, and carry you off the court.

▲

After practicing the above visualization for several weeks, try visualizing yourself in a sexual situation actually getting the erection you desire with a partner. See an image of your body as it responds to arousal. Image the movements, sounds, and pleasure you anticipate the situation would bring. Allow yourself, in your mind, to get into the experience as a full participant, not a spectator. Practice this visualization many times until you feel you've become an ''expert'' in achieving an erection. Once you become an expert you can replay your personal video at any time. The more you practice this visualization, the more confidence you'll have in the real situation.

There are two other causes of erection difficulties that need to be mentioned. Although these causes are not as remote as the ones mentioned above, too often they are overlooked as contributors to sexual difficulties.

Inappropriate or Insufficient Stimulation from a Partner

A young adult male usually has many spontaneous erections, sometimes embarrassingly so. As he matures, however, the spontaneous nature of his erections decreases. Because it takes more visual and/or direct erotic stimulation to achieve an erection, he may not be getting sufficient stimulation.

In healthy males, this change is insidious and does not seem to have a fixed point when it actually happens. Yet, some men seem to experience the change suddenly, depending on the circumstances of the man's life. An overreaction to this change can create the self-fullfilling, performance anxiety described above. Self-conscious about not having an immediate erection, a man might begin to watch or monitor his arousal—something he probably never did in his youth. His concentration is now out of the immediate moment and experiencing pleasurable sensations becomes impossible. The cycle begins.

It's not unusual for a man who has these expectations of himself to connect up with a partner who also expects him to have spontaneous erections. Perhaps at one time in the relationship, foreplay wasn't "necessary" for arousal. The erection always "appeared" on the scene at the appropriate time. Then when things begin to change, the partner is caught off guard. What happened to the automatic erection? Never having done much to contribute to the erection, a partner may either be unwilling to directly stimulate the man or uncomfortable touching male genitals. At the other extreme, I've met men who were so "proud" of their previous spontaneous erection capacity that they felt insulted by the suggestion that a partner "help" them get an erection.

Sometimes the problem can be corrected by educating the couple about effective foreplay techniques. However, it's more likely that this situation has resulted in the development of a classic case of loss of concentration and then performance anxiety. The solution, again, becomes regaining concentration.

Not Wanting to Be There in the First Place

When it comes to sex, our culture has passed along to men some destructive myths about sexuality and masculinity. Too often men insist on being in sexual situations that aren't right for them. Sometimes it's because they feel the pressure to act on any sexual opportunity presented to them, in marriage or in casual relationships. Turning down sex somehow seems emasculating. Sometimes they don't know how to say no because they may fear hurting someone's feelings. And sometimes they refuse to believe that they actually need to be attracted to a partner to get turned on. Our culture has led them to believe their arousal response *should* be invincible. These are the situations in which their body refuses to be controlled by a belief system based on masculine myths. The penis, being wiser than cultural tradition, simply says, ''I won't work for a boss that demands I do what isn't good for me.''

Sometimes not wanting to be there can be more global than sex. It can mean not wanting to be in the relationship (see chapter 8). Not wanting to be in the relationship you're in often feels like being in prison. Rarely is there an uncomplicated escape route in which someone doesn't get badly hurt, emotionally, financially, or both. Feeling sexually aroused is difficult when one feels trapped by only negative choices.

Lubrication and Swelling Difficulties in Women

Physical. Certain illnesses are also known to be responsible for arousal difficulties in women. This area has received less attention and less research than with male arousal so there is less known about female arousal problems. This results in a tendency to dismiss problems as purely psychological. A woman, therefore, needs to be carefully examined and questioned by a knowledgeable healthcare person. It is known that trauma to the genital area through injury, surgery, or repeated infections can create permanent problems. Both prescription and recreational drugs are also known to inhibit sexual response.

Psychological. Interestingly enough, when it comes to arousal problems, men and women are not all that different. The effect of all psychological arousal problems for women is also a loss of concentration. The deeper causes for loss concentration are the same as for men:

- Fear of psychological pain, which blocks pleasure (see chapter 7)
- Inability to balance own pleasure with needing to please and perform (see chapter 7)

- Feelings of guilt and shame surrounding lust and/or pleasure (see chapters 5 and 7)
- Fear of failure as a result of a previous failure
- Inappropriate or ineffective sexual stimulation (see chapter 9)
- Not wanting to be there in the first place (see chapter 9)

Any difference in the deeper causes for arousal problems between men and women is more likely to be one of emphasis. The differences are almost always cultural artifacts. For example, women are more likely to have feelings of guilt around lust because men are expected and, therefore, given permission to be sexual; women, on the other hand, are expected to be pure. Also, the number of women who have problems because of inadequate stimulation is higher than with men. This is because women tend to be the more passive partner, either not knowing what they need in the way of stimulation or feeling inhibited about asking. It also seems to be the case that women more often fall prey to needing to please whereas men more often fall prey to needing to perform.

When a woman loses the ability to concentrate on pleasure, her body talks to her too. It says the same thing as a man's, "I won't work for a boss that demands I do what isn't good for me." When we ask our bodies to ignore something that isn't right, they talk back to us. Sometimes they signal us with pain, as when we physically abuse them. With sex, our bodies simply "walk off the job." Instead of becoming aroused, they shut down—go on strike, so-to-speak. There is no rush of blood to the genitals and there is no lubrication as a result of increased blood supply to the area. It's the body's protective way of insisting we pay attention to the deeper causes. As with men, the inability to become aroused is an anxiety warning sign.

To correct the problem, a woman must be able to concentrate on pleasurable sensations. Her focus must be in the moment. Use the following visualization to help regain the ability to stay with pleasurable sensations.

▼

Steam Heat

It's been a hectic day during which you've been pulled in many different directions. Your organizational skills have been tested to the max. It's late afternoon and you decide to take a long soak in a hot tub before the evening meal. You undress and slowly lower yourself into the hot water. As each inch of your body is lowered into the water, you feel your troubles fading away. All you feel is the tingling of your skin as it comes in contact with the water. Your eyes are closed and you concentrate on the soothing feel of the warmth. The steam is reaching up to your face and creating beads of sweat, which clean your system of your troubles. Suddenly, the ringing of the phone breaks your concentration. Immediately, you feel your muscles tense up. Your first instinct is to get out of the tub and answer the phone. It could be something very important.

Instead, you turn your attention back to the feel of the hot water on your skin. As you focus on the soothing feeling of the water, your muscles relax again and the ringing of the phone fades away. It's just you, your skin, and the feel of the water. You're able to completely block out the ringing sound. You continue to let your body relax and your mind stay on the calming effect of the water.

You feel a great sense of peace and tranquility as you merge with the sensations of the water on your skin. In time, the water begins to cool and you come back to the real world, feeling refreshed and alive.

▲

After practicing the above visualization many times, try visualizing yourself becoming aroused with a partner. Cast yourself as the star and picture you and your partner making love. See your body respond in the manner you want. Image every little detail of how you would like to be. In your mind, become an expert at becoming sexually aroused. Get so familiar with how responsive you can be, that the real situation becomes a snap because you've done it so many times before.

Problems with the Plateau Phase

As mentioned above, the plateau phase of the sexual response cycle varies from individual to individual and even from one situation to the next within an individual's experience. After becoming sexually excited, a person's arousal may level off for a few seconds, one minute, five minutes, thirty minutes, or more. The ability to concentrate on pleasure during the plateau phase determines the length of time elapsing before orgasm. If we learn how to monitor pleasure during this phase, we can fine-tune our ability to move more or less rapidly through the phase.

Premature Orgasm

In this situation, the plateau phase is cut short. Orgasm occurs immediately after sexual excitement. There is no pause in the cycle to allow for the building of sexual tension. Consequently, the orgasm phase feels muted, less intense.

Premature orgasm occurs in both men and women, although men seem much more prone to have this problem than women. The immediate cause of premature orgasm is anxiety, which inhibits concentration on pleasure. Instead of monitoring pleasure, the person monitors orgasm, trying to prevent the orgasm from happening too quickly. In the process he or she bypasses the plateau phase. The most appropriate analogy is the athlete who "jumps the gun" at the starting line. This happens because the athlete is thinking about the outcome instead of concentrating in the moment. The deeper causes for premature orgasm are the same as for other phases of the response cycle.

By focusing on pleasure, the plateau phase is allowed to run its natural course rather than being "cut off at the pass." Use this visualization to focus on pleasure.

* * *

Pleasure Station

Imagine that your maximum pleasure is like a frequency on your own radio. Your radio is special because once you tune in to your point of maximum pleasure, it goes away and you won't be able to tune in again for a few hours. On either side of the maximum point are points of intense pleasure. The object is to stay on either side of the maximum point until you're ready.

You're fine-tuning your pleasure by turning the knob to the right or left without letting it reach the exact frequency. This takes intense focusing. Because your concentration is so intense, you can move it a little to the right or left and keep it away from its maximum point. You've got control over reaching the maximum point because you're focused in the moment. If you get distracted, you realize how easy it would be to prematurely hit the maximum point. You get to stay at the verge of pleasure until you decide that you want to hit the maximum point.

Problems with the Orgasm Phase

The orgasm phase is triggered by an involuntary reflex. Because of its involuntary nature, it cannot be controlled by our conscious mind. We cannot "will" an orgasm. Orgasm happens as a result of the buildup of appropriate erotic stimulation. If we stop, even for a moment, focusing on erotic pleasure, the buildup drops and the reflex is not triggered. Sometimes it only drops slightly whereas other times it may bottom out. Continued stimulation at this point may lose its pleasurable association if focusing remains distracted.

Reaching the trigger point requires a momentary abandonment of conscious awareness, sometimes called a flow state (see chapter 1). During this period, awareness remains totally focused on sensations. This total abandonment means letting go of conscious control. For some people, the idea of being out of control for even a few moments produces anxiety. Thus, the conscious mind "fights" the loss of control with nonerotic thoughts. A very typical distracting (and nonerotic) thought that prevents triggering orgasm is, "How come it's taking so long?" Once the mind has switched to watching the clock, it becomes increasingly difficult to empty the mind of timekeeping and fill it up with either erotic sensations or images. It becomes a case of "don't think about pink elephants." The suggestion creates a self-fullfilling prophecy.

The causes for not wanting to lose control are the same as the deeper causes that interfere with the other phases. However, of particular significance to orgasm difficulties are the fear of psychological pain as a result of abandonment and feelings of guilt and shame surrounding lust.

Both men and women have problems with reaching orgasm. Women, however, far outnumber men in reporting this problem. Women, because of a history of economic dependence on men, have greater fears of abandonment. As explained in chapter 5, they also have more guilt about lust than men do. These facts explain why women are more prone than men to orgasm difficulties. It would be a mistake, though, to assume orgasm difficulties are rare in men. The truth is that men who have this problem rarely fess up to it so the numbers are obscured by the lack of reporting.

Another important consideration for women who have orgasm problems has to do with receiving effective stimulation. As you remember, the orgasm reflex is triggered by a *buildup* of erotic stimulation. Some women need more time for this buildup than other women and, generally, more buildup time than men. Not surprisingly, then, some women never receive either enough stimulation or the right kind of stimulation to build up to orgasm. Losing control to sensations won't produce orgasms if the sensations are either not pleasurable or don't last long enough to move through the plateau phase to the orgasm phase.

Communication between partners is essential if each is to receive the kind and amount of erotic stimulation they need to build up to the orgasm phase. Chapters 3 and 8 discuss the importance of communication and provide some visualizations that enhance verbal communication between partners.

If you're having trouble letting go of control and totally abandoning yourself to erotic pleasure, use this visualization to help you let go.

* * *

The Slide of Your Life

Imagine you have climbed several hundred feet to the top of one of those giant water slides. You felt a great thrill and anticipation with each step you climb. You know the ride down is going to be fantastic. Everyone in front of you is having the experience of a lifetime and you want to experience it too.

You've reached the top and it's your turn to head down. You're sitting there, holding on and looking down at the distance. You feel reluctant to just let go. You know if you just stop holding yourself back, the forward momentum will take you on a natural course of intense excitement and pleasure as your body hurls itself downward. You realize it takes only a split second to make the decision to turn your body over to the experience. Others in front of you have done it and have shouted with exhilaration and joy. You, too, want to sense the abandonment, the freedom of letting the moment of pleasure overtake any fears you have. You let go and you're off on the ride of your life.

After practicing this visualization for several weeks, try visualizing yourself in a sexual situation actually having an orgasm with a partner. See an image of your body as it totally lets go. Image the movements, sounds, and pleasure you anticipate an orgasm would bring. Allow yourself, in your mind, to get into the experience as a full participant. Practice this visualization many times until you feel you've become an "expert" in having a visual orgasm. Once you become an expert you can replay your personal video at any time. The practicing in your mind will make the real situation seem easy.

The Solution Is in Your Right Brain Where You Learn to Concentrate

At the symptom level, the goal is to regain concentration on erotic sensations and to experience pleasure. If focusing becomes difficult, sexual fantasy can be extremely effective in overpowering distractions. You'll remember from chapter 4 that fantasy has the ability to enhance eroticism. Erotic images keep the mind in the right brain and, therefore, help concentration. In one sense, sexual fantasy "distracts the distractor."

Sexual fantasy is especially useful with symptoms of the excitement and orgasm phases. If we're blocking arousal, as in erection or lubrication difficulties, sexual fantasy "hurdles" the blocks. If we're having problems reaching the peak of the orgasm phase, sexual fantasy "boosts" us up and over the top.

We all have the capacity for fantasizing. For some of us it seems easy and natural. For others it seems more like work. Like anything we're unfamiliar with, however, practice eventually makes it seem natural. If you want to enhance your sexuality through the use of sexual fantasy, read and practice the visualizations in chapter 4.

When to Consult a Professional and How to Make a Decision on Who's Best for You

The roadblocks to sexual enjoyment are numerous. As I've said many times, in a culture as sexuality-phobic as ours, no one has a clear, straight path to healthy adult sexuality. The visualizations in this book are designed to help you remove or overcome the various roadblocks that are in your way to fantastic sex. With repeated practice over time, you should see some dramatic results.

Sometimes, however, the roadblocks remain resistant to change. Usually this is because we have incorrectly identified them or have skipped ahead without removing a previous one. As you can tell from the cases presented in this book, roadblocks can be very tricky and devious; they look and feel like something different from what they are. It becomes possible, then, to attempt to use a visualization that doesn't hit the mark. We may also miss the mark by getting too far ahead of ourselves. That is, we may try to alleviate a symptom before we've dealt with a deeper cause. In both of these situations, the visualizations may not be effective.

Well-trained professionals can help us identify the roadblocks in our way to satisfying sex. They can also help us know if we're trying to skip over a block. Sometimes we skip over blocks because they're too painful to deal with. If this is the case, a good therapist can be supportive and caring in assisting you through the pain.

Early traumatic experiences such as physical or sexual abuse or loss of a parent have significant effects on our ability to abandon ourselves to sexual pleasure. Visualizations can be very effective in letting go of the pain. They're simple to do and anyone can do them. However, they do have to be guided in the right direction and ordered according to hierarchy of resistance.

Cindy's situation in chapter 8 is a perfect example. She easily visualized her guilt about sex as a ball and chain, but was unable to see herself letting go of this guilt without first seeing herself as deserving of pleasure. One had to come before the other. Cindy knew about her guilt, but it took professional help for her to understand what was blocking her way. By going back far enough, in this case visualizing being reborn, Cindy was able to remove the hurdles to her sexual pleasure.

What to Look for in a Professional

A good sex therapist is first and foremost a good therapist. Although there are always exceptions to every rule, you're much safer if you see only a licensed therapist. A license if *not* a guarantee that your therapist knows what he or she is doing, it's only a first step in the elimination process.

Getting a recommendation from somebody you trust increases the probability that you'll end up in good hands. Unfortunately, when it comes to sexual issues, few friends will volunteer that they've been in therapy. Your next best bet is to consult your family doctor. You'll have to be brave and bring it up. Most doctors will not ask about your sexual happiness during a routine visit. If there is a major university in your area, they may have a department of human sexuality that may be able to give you a referral in your area.

In the United States, there is an organization that certifies sex therapists. The organization is called the American Association of Sex Educators, Counselors, and Therapists. (AASECT) Their office is located at 435 North Michigan Avenue, Suite 1717, Chicago, Illinois 60611–4067; (312) 644-0828. They publish a directory of therapists who have been specially trained to deal with sexual problems. Again, although it is no guarantee that you'll get somebody who is good, a therapist certified as a sex therapist will have had training and supervision in sexual problems. It's another step in the elimination process.

In addition to ensuring that the therapist you select is licensed as a therapist and certified as a sex therapist, you need to trust your intuition. You must feel comfortable with your therapist. If after several visits, you still don't feel comfortable, keep searching. It's a good idea to shop for a therapist until you find the right "fit" for you.

Therapy is a situation that is designed to talk about *you*. Your therapist should be there to listen to you. It's appropriate for a therapist to reveal himself or herself only if it's relevant to your situation. Don't put up with a therapist who spends more time talking about himself or herself than about you. A therapist should not talk on the phone during your time either. *And never allow a therapist to engage you in any sexual contact.* Any kind of nudity or sex between a patient and therapist is both inappropriate and unethical. Sex therapy patients are vulnerable when it comes to sex and a therapist should never take advantage of this situation.

Not all sex therapists use visualization as a therapeutic tool. It's appropriate and legitimate for you to ask them about it if you're interested in working further with visualizations. It's also appropriate to ask them to read this book. I've had many patients share wonderful books with me that have broadened my scope of therapeutic skills.

▼

Epilogue

▲

Even in the last decade of a century where we noncha-
lantly watch explicit sex on a large public screen, we
remain, at a very private level, unsophisticated, uncomfortable, and silent about our own sexuality. Quietly and
privately, we all struggle with sexual questions, insecu-
rities, and curiosities. What does the aggression in our
sexual fantasies mean? Are our turn-ons normal? Is our
desire average? Are we good lovers? Without meaning
to, we take these uncertainties into the bedroom with us
where they all too often sabotage our yearning for sexual
intimacy and satisfaction.

We certainly don't intend to undermine our goal. So
how is it that it happens? Because we're unknowingly
stuck with negative images from our past. To have true
sexual intimacy, we need to leave behind images of sex
as sinful, dirty, shameful, undignified, conquering, and
sexist. We need to replace these with images of sex as
nurturing, pleasurable, playful, lustful, loving, and mutual. With these images as our companions, we have a
chance at making a long-term, satisfying, intimately sexual relationship work.

Visualization is a way to both discover what images
hold us back from reaching our goals and to replace old
images with new ones. It is simple to do, requires only
ourselves, takes very little time, doesn't cost a thing, and

works! We couldn't ask for a more economic, efficient tool for change. The only catch is that as with all change, it has to be practiced for it to make a difference.

Many of the mysteries of the mind remain unsolved. It's principally a theoretical concept that different mental functions operate from two distinct sides of our brain. It's not theoretical, however, that imagery acts as a powerful guide, leading our behavior in one direction or another. It's also clear, that by directing imagery through visualization, we can act as our *own* guide and go in a chosen direction. When we do, we shake loose the past negative influences and start with a clean slate. It's at that point that we have the opportunity to write our own ticket to sexual happiness.

▼

Appendix

▲

Index of Visualizations

For easy reference, the visualizations in this book are listed below along with each visualization's purpose. Refer to this index if you have a specific goal you are working on or if you want to refresh your memory on a particular visualization.

▼

References

▲

Chapter 1

1. Bay, Adelaide. *Visualization: Directing the Movie of Your Mind.* New York: Barnes and Noble, 1978.
2. Khatena, Joe. *Imagery and Creative Imagination.* Buffalo, N.Y.: Bearly Limited, 1984.
3. Leckart, Bruce. *Up from Boredom, Down from Fear.* New York: Richard Marek Publisher, 1980.
4. Sheikh, Anees, ed. *The Potential of Fantasy and Imagination.* New York: Brandon House, 1979.
5. Klinger, Eric. *Structure and Function of Fantasy.* New York: Wiley-Interscience, 1971.
6. "Going with the Flow." *Newsweek,* June 2, 1986, 68.
7. Roberts, Marjory. "Be All That You Can Be" (special report). *Psychology Today,* March 1988, 28–29.
8. Springer, Sally, and Georg Deutsch. *Left Brain, Right Brain.* San Francisco: W. H. Freeman and Co., 1981.
9. Geschwind, Norman, ed. *Cerebral Dominance.* Cambridge, Mass.: Harvard University Press, 1984.
10. Morris, Peter E., and Peter Hampson. *Imagery and Consciousness.* New York and London: Academic Press, 1983.

227

11. Kosslyn, Stephen. *Ghosts in the Mind's Machine: Creating and Using Images in the Brain.* New York and London: W. W. Norton and Co., 1983.

Chapter 2

1. Humphries, Christmas. *Concentration and Meditation.* Santa Fe, N. Mex.: Sun Publishing, 1981.
2. Thompson, Keith. "Concentration." *Esquire,* May 1984, 131–132.
3. "How Your Memory Works." *Wellness Letter.* Berkeley, Calif.: University of California, 5(1) (October 1988).

Chapter 3

1. Goodall, Jane. *In the Shadow of Man.* New York: Dell Publishing, 1971.

Chapter 4

1. Money, John. *Lovemaps.* New York: Irvington Publishers, Inc., 1986.
2. Barbach, Lonnie. *For Yourself: The Fulfillment of Female Sexuality.* New York, New American Library, 1975.
3. Nass, Gilbert, Roger W. Libby, and Mary Pat Fisher. *Sexual Choices.* Monterey, Calif.: Wadsworth Health Science Division, 1981.
4. Masters, R. E., ed. *Sexual Self-Stimulation.* Los Angeles: Sherbourne Press, Inc., 1967.

Chapter 5

1. Chereb, David M. *Night Dreams.* Lake Forest, Calif.: Merz Productions, 1986.
2. Money, John. *Lovemaps.* New York: Irvington Publishers, Inc., 1986.

3. Jones, Stanley. "The Biological Origin of Love and Hate." In *Feelings and Emotions,* edited by Magna Aronold. New York and London: Academic Press, 1970.
4. Masters, R. E., ed. *Sexual Self-Stimulation.* Los Angeles: Sherbourne Press, Inc., 1967.

Chapter 6

1. Caplan, Frank, and Theresa Caplan. *The Power of Play.* New York: Anchor Press, Doubleday, 1973.
2. Hill, Lyda, and Nancy L. Smith. "Humor and Play" in *Self-Care Nursing.* East Norwalk, Conn.: Appleton & Lange, 1985.
3. McLellan, Joyce. *The Question of Play.* Elmsford, N.Y.: Pergamon Press, 1970.
4. Winnicott, D. W. *Playing and Reality.* London: Tavistock Publications, 1971.

Chapter 9

1. Masters, William H., and Virginia E. Johnson. *Human Sexual Response.* Boston: Little, Brown & Co., 1966.

Index